HEALTH, HOLINESS & WHOLENESS FOR
MINISTRY LEADERS

John R. Matthews
with Kristina R. Gutiérrez
and Ross D. Peterson

Foreword by Stephen Ott

D0870280

JUDSON PRESS
PUBLISHERS SINCE 1824
VALLEY FORGE, PA

Judson Press has made every effort to trace the ownership of all quotes. In the event of a question arising from the use of a quote, we regret any error made and will be pleased to make the necessary correction in future printings and editions of this book.

Note: All names and identifying information of the clients described have been changed to protect their privacy.

Interior design by Wendy Ronga / Hampton Design Group.
Cover design by Lisa Delgado, Delgado and Company, Inc.

Library of Congress Cataloging-in-Publication data
Names: Matthews, John Richard, author. | Gutiérrez, Kristina R., author. | Peterson, Ross D., author. Title: Health, holiness, and wholeness for ministry leaders / John R. Matthews with Kristina R. Gutierrez and Ross D. Peterson; foreword by Stephen Ott. Identifiers: LCCN 2019046341 (print) | LCCN 2019046342 (ebook) | ISBN 9780817018092 (paperback) | ISBN 9780817082086 (epub) Subjects: LCSH: Clergy—Health and hygiene. | Pastoral theology. | Church work. Classification: LCC BV4397.5 .M38 2020 (print) | LCC BV4397.5 (ebook) | DDC 253/.2—dc23 LC record available at https://lccn.loc.gov/2019046341LC ebook record available at https://lccn.loc.gov/2019046342 Printed in the U.S.A.

First printing, 2020.

Contents

Foreword

Ministry is a challenging vocation, demanding a wide range of skills, personal ability, mature wisdom, systems awareness, and consistent practical judgment. These foundational abilities are energized and sustained by developing a healthy and satisfying personal life. The vocational and interpersonal casualty rate among ministers is high, and proficient guidance is not always easy to find. We need nurturing and realistic materials and for consultation, recognizing and dealing with the growth and formation needs of ministers at all stages of vocational lifecycle.

John (Jay) Matthews and two of his colleagues at Midwest Ministry Development Service have put together just such a book for ministers. Jay refers to it as a "training manual for your inner coach." But a training manual to do what? This book is an earnest and practical invitation for the inner and outer practices of health, excellence, and ministry. It is not an academic book, and there is no scholarly bibliography at the end. Instead, it is based on Jay's decades of experience and reflection on the practice of ministry, drawing on his learnings of the enduring qualities from "the brightest and best" pastors he encountered.

Jay shares with the reader practical guidance, tips for healthy attitude and boundary formation, and options for creative longevity in ministry. Many of his clients over the years have been well-functioning persons who sought vocational renewal, self-examination, and a "second breath" in their stage of vocation. Others were persons experiencing difficulty, conflict, burnout, or repeated disappointing and draining experiences in their work. He discusses the roots of those various challenges. Jay describes the habits, attitudes, and practices that make for living out excellence, creativity, and authenticity for each person engaged in ministry leadership.

This book is about formation for ministry. Jay writes that formation is a continuing and unfolding story throughout one's life and vocation; many issues appear repeatedly in one's lifecycle, though perhaps in different guises and circumstances. Sometimes the core principles Matthews identifies are missed or glossed in the training and habit formation part of vocational development. Conversely, some problems of personal brokenness, missing skills, problematic attitudes or habits, or reactivity surface only after years of experience, and these require a sensitive and skillful intervention and correction.

One of the best parts of the book is the section that discusses differentiating Self and Role, for they are not interchangeable. Indeed, they become dangerous to ministry practice when they merge. Jay rightly points out that the area of healthy overlap between Self and Role is where continuing growth and renewal is likely to happen. His discussion of developing and practicing a sense of proper ethical and behavioral boundaries is also quite important in ministry leadership. His Principles of Excellence are a critical contribution toward increasing well-being in the minister and in their leadership. He increases the practical value of these concepts by offering concrete exercises for the reader to undertake.

The book is invaluable to persons still in the basic training phase of ministry formation, especially if they are in dialogue with a mentor in ministry. The book will be instructive for judicatory personnel, highlighting areas of pastoral high-functioning and areas of problematic behavior, to enhance conversations with supervising persons. The book would also be helpful to seasoned, mid-career ministers (and later) as they search for areas of growth, healing, or deeper understanding of themselves.

—Rev. Stephen Ott, PhD

Preface

One of the important purposes of a Preface is to potentially stop people from reading the book. After all, if it's not what you expected or needed or wanted, why bother? So, I offer this Preface hoping to help you make that decision by giving you a glimpse of what this book is about.

The process of writing this book was fun, but also worrisome. I worried about the idea that as someone writing about excellence, I might be expected to exemplify it myself and demonstrate it on every page. I worried that this was turning out to be a "how to" book. I was telling myself that scholars don't write "how to" books; they write "what really is" books.

Then I worried that so much of the book starts with "I." I had even hoped to avoid the use of the first-person pronoun or voice altogether. I soon found it is impossible, since I frequently told stories of my encounters with my "brightest and best." I also repeated much of what I had been doing in the workshops on the topic—the whole purpose of writing the book in the first place. There, I felt less inhibited and more natural in using the first person.

As I started to read what I had written, I worried that it was a bit "all over the place." I calmed myself with the reminder that all authors put something of their own strengths into the way they write and, inadvertently, their quirks and weaknesses as well. I apologize and, in advance, thank you for the extra effort you may need to invest in order to follow along.

One thing I did not worry about was my intent. Wanting to raise the caliber of ministry in the church seemed like a worthy enough aim. However, I also had all the confidence in the world in my former clients whose stunning virtues I sought to make accessible to everyone working on behalf of God in the pulpit, classroom, youth lounge, prison cell, hospital room, bishop's chair, mission field, and street corner—those whom I call my "brightest and best." These people have been my daily company for the last forty years and have made my life rich, fulfilling, and interesting. It has been a privilege to support ministers as they seek to give the best of themselves to the church.

As for fun, I have always known it was my responsibility to make my workshops both substantial (with enough serious content that participants find them worthwhile to attend) and fun. I even resort to such strategies as tossing out a trivia question prior to a break so that the introverts who find it uncomfortable to mingle with a bunch of strangers will have something to talk about. With this book, I continue the attempt to mix substance with fun. I sincerely hope that does not detract from my very serious intent to share the lessons learned from exceptional ministers in order to improve the health and excellence of all those in ministry.

This book is based on a number of workshops that I have led as a part of my work at Midwest Ministry Development on the topic of "Health and Excellence in Ministry." The purpose of those workshops is to motivate those who attend to take very seriously the importance of developing healthy behavior patterns in their ministries while aiming for the best ministry they are capable of providing. This book, much of which is taken from my workshop notes, has a workshop flavor. Even though I developed an important theoretical base for the trainings, the content often turned practical and specific: How do you deal with gossip? How do you deal with routine pastoral calls? When and how do you tell people you are leaving the church or organization?

Most of the wisdom in this book is second-hand, gleaned from clients with whom I was privileged to spend time, and much of the workshop material includes my first-hand accounts of interactions with them. Some of those individuals, as they talked in depth about their experience, gave me eye-opening accounts of ministry done extremely well—far beyond what I would have imagined. Others provided me with an abundance of "what not to do" stories. I wanted to distill all of that and share it with new candidates for ministry. I also wanted this project to be a resource to those who are already active in ministry but may be surprised by the difficulties of day-to-day life in the church.

Needless to say, the attempt here is not exhaustive. What I've learned from those who have made the concept of health and excellence in ministry come to life has been distilled into a few recommendations that essentially hold together as one approach, though certainly not the only one.

This is not a medical book. While physical and mental health are noted as important, *health* is primarily used as relating to behaviors or behavior patterns. The concept of *wholeness* figures prominently in the way health is considered. A healthy body is one in which all the parts are working together as a *whole*. The same model applies to behavior. The healthiest behaviors are engaged in *whole*heartedly. When you put your whole self into something, your work becomes lighter and more enjoyable.

In contrast, the things you do with indifference or ambivalence entail "fighting yourself," draining much more energy, dulling your morale, and producing a weakened effect. To do something wholeheartedly is a choice you make—not always an easy one. One of the most important specific junctures ahead is the description of how you can set things up so that it is easy—almost automatic—to choose wholehearted behaviors in your day-to-day ministry.

Excellence in relation to ministry, regardless of the setting, is also considered in a particular way. Parish ministry can be divided into several component areas of proficiency: preaching, biblical knowledge, pastoral counseling, advocacy, and justice work. Measurement standards can be approached for each. Excellence is sometimes defined as high marks in all or a vast majority of those areas. The concept of excellence in this book, however, has nothing to do with elitism or ego. It is something that is available to anyone committed to certain ways of doing ministry. Chapter 8 provides a deeper exploration of the meaning of excellence in ministry.

What is meant by *ministry* in the context of this book? I draw my concept of ministry from the clients for whom I've put on workshops. My clients over the years have included bishops, seminary and college professors, hospital chaplains, military chaplains, candidates for ordained ministry, and a host of other ministerial specializations. However, even though the overwhelming majority of my clients have been ordained clergy and congregational pastors, I believe that the material in this book applies to all who believe that any part of their lives, at any time, can be thought of as ministry, whether that is ministry to your family through daily chores or consoling a grieving friend.

So, can *health, excellence,* and *ministry* really co-exist for those living a life in ministry? Don't these three terms pull one in very different directions? The answer found in these pages is that they not only can exist together, they actually thrive together. There actually is a path to levels of personal and vocational health and excellence that you never thought were possible!

PART 1

The Setting

CHAPTER 1

The Brightest and Best

For the past forty years it has been my daily work, and my privilege, to sit down and talk with people doing ministry. Early on I learned that some do ministry better than others, and some do it amazingly well. They do it so well that even when they talk about their failures, I'm impressed—even thrilled—that they reflect such a clear channel for God to work through. And, at the same time, they seem to fulfill what God must surely want for all of us. They seem supremely happy—not always an obvious happiness, but a joy that runs strong and comes from a deep source. I would meet with them for only two or three days, but they were hard to forget, and I came to think of them as "my brightest and best."

I want to communicate what I learned from my clients, but I know that professional ethics keep me from sharing anything but very general information about these exceptional ministers—nothing that would make them recognizable. I also know they are such a diverse group of unique individuals that, even if I could talk about each of them by name, it would be a challenge to distill their collective wisdom into a single unity.

But I must tell what I can about some of my brightest and best. One of the earliest and most memorable was someone I'll call Colin (to protect the identities of my clients, I'll be using false names throughout). I met Colin in the early 1970s when I conducted a weeklong workshop in Canada. Among the ten participants, Colin, at age fifty-five, was at least a decade older than the others. What I learned of Colin during the introductions was that he did not like to sit still (though he seemed composed and at ease throughout the week), he put together his sermons on the run, and he spent most of his time either playing hockey or talking with people in bars. One night late in the week, the group stayed around afterward and got into a lively bull session. The topic was the stinginess of their churches, and it became heated, going from "no cost-of-living raise," to "no raise at all," to "actual cuts in pay." The group agreed that church councils are totally insensitive to the needs of their ministers and their ministers' families.

Everyone chimed in—except Colin, who remained uncharacteristically silent throughout the session. I commented to him about this afterward, and he told me that he had sat there feeling embarrassed. He had not wanted to share with the group the battle he had recently fought with his church council. His council had demanded that he accept a ten-thousand-dollar raise! He had argued that they could not afford it and that, if they wanted to spend that kind of money, many mission projects were far more worthy. He lost the battle.

I surmised that Colin must be doing something special that his council recognized as excellent ministry. Colin invited me to go to lunch with him at the school cafeteria, and of course I accepted. While we were standing in line, he excused himself and walked over to a young male student. I was not close enough to hear their words, but I observed that something out of the ordinary was taking place. Even though they obviously were not telling jokes, their faces were animated and a warmth seemed to be passing between them. It was as if the forty-year difference in their ages did not exist. Colin displayed an absolute lack of phoniness, an absence of the kind of stiffness I've seen in other ministers in similar situations. I knew real pastoral care had taken place in a conversation that lasted only four minutes at best. I later asked him if that student was someone he knew well. He response: "Oh no, he is someone who has come to our church a couple of times. I've never spoken to him before, and I just wanted to say hello."

Years later, a woman I'll call Natalie came to my office, and she prompted me to go back and revisit that moment with Colin in the cafeteria. On the day she came for her required candidate evaluation, I was feeling miserable and out of sorts. After my initial one-hour session with her, I felt on top of the world—a remarkable and welcome transformation. I later checked with the staff psychologist who also met with her, and he reported the same experience.

This time I set out to try to understand how Natalie had this impact on others. It was not that she had said anything complimentary to me, nothing that would have boosted my ego. What I did discover is what I have come to call "immediacy," a quality high on my list of desirable things to look for in candidates and a quality worth developing if you desire excellence in ministry. She was fully present in the moment, as if the freshness of the immediate experience offered unlimited possibilities unbound by anything in the past. She spoke to me in an unguarded, spontaneous way and listened deeply, as if she wanted to use all her faculties to hear and understand what I was saying. She allowed her feelings, at every moment congruent with what she was saying, to show that she was **there** with me, and nowhere else. During that hour, all that mattered was our conversation. I felt cared for and ministered to, and I concluded that she was an excellent representative of God's love. I also wondered how she exhibited such immediacy even in the face of the anxiety that typically accompanies candidates coming in for evaluation.

Absence of Self-Concern

Not long after that experience with Natalie, I received a call from a denominational official, a bishop whom I had come to know well. He had decided he wanted more balance in how he attended to the pastors in his jurisdiction. He was aware that he had been spending almost all his time and energy on those pastors who seemed to attract trouble, at the expense of other pastors who were serving well. He decided to do something special for those other pastors. He invited about a dozen of them to a special gathering to honor and celebrate their faithful contribution to God's work in the world. He invited me to come and be a part of the event, and he gave me freedom to do whatever I wanted. What I wanted to do was seize this golden opportunity to increase my understanding of excellence in ministry. I was open with them about my agenda and simply asked them to talk freely about how they go about their work, including their intents, their fears, what they look for, and what they attempt to avoid.

I don't know what I was expecting, but I came out very grateful for having found a striking commonality among them, one that would become a cornerstone of what I would come to speak and write about as "excellence in ministry." As I write about it here, consider it a preview of the First Principle of Excellence. What I found in each of their accounts was a complete **absence of self-concern.** If, as individuals, they had any concern about being noticed, liked, approved of, or thought of as clever or secure in their jobs, they consistently managed to keep that concern **out** of what they did in ministry. And it made all the difference in the world!

My brief encounters with Colin and Natalie, memorable though they were, cannot begin to convey the scope of what I have found in my clients who exhibit excellence. Two things in general can be said about the brightest and best. First, the work they do is remarkable. Their intentions for their ministries are well thought out and made clear to all. What's more, what they have intended is consistently close to their results. They expect a lot of themselves and of their people. In this day and age, when boundaries have been firmly encouraged in the work of ministry, they relate to their people in ways that are neither distant nor formal, warm but quite distinct from friendship. They have done things that have gained the trust and respect of their people. And, in one sense, they take advantage of that, using that relational currency to stretch and challenge the people to go deeper into their faith and further with their mission. In another sense, they would never take advantage of the trust they have built; they would not use it in any way for their personal gain.

Second, is that their high-quality and excellent ministry relates to all spheres of their health—physical, emotional, relational, and spiritual. One of the most striking things about these excellent ministers, as I mentioned, is that they are happy. The outward sign is that they smile easily and often. Of course, these character-istics contribute to their excellence—to a degree that is hard to overestimate. But these characteristics are also indications of a robust health that can be spelled out in many ways: practices, atti-tudes, and the way they go about conducting ministry. To them, health and excellence are very much tied together. What supports one, supports the other.

How Did They Get There?

The real question is not so much what these shining stars of min-istry do but how they got there. To answer this question, I need to go back to what I learned from the bishop's group of best min-isters. At first these ministers seemed like an ordinary group of people, but I gradually realized that their conversation had a dif-ferent quality than what I usually heard when ministers talk about their work. It finally became clear to me: very little ego was involved in what they were saying. They did not take themselves seriously at all, while at the same time they took their work extremely seriously and expected a great deal of themselves. It wasn't that they seemed to be working harder or longer. It was more their obvious enjoyment in what they were doing that made them seem lighter and happier. The key was the almost total absence of self-concern in their ministries. That putting aside of self-concern opened the door for some pretty amazing things to happen.

From then on I realized that some foundational principles could be far more valuable to my mission than an array of case studies or role models. Principles could be shared, while the details of case studies could not. The problem with using role models is that we end up focusing on outward appearances, and we miss the heart and soul of what is truly worth having. Role models imply a put-down of yourself: "Here is someone better than you, so you should be like that person." Principles, on the other hand, give you something to grasp and apply in your own way, leaving the best unique parts of yourself respected and intact. What I learned from the bishop's best—the separation of self-concern from the pastor's work role—seemed to be the root of what I later came to think of as **purity of ministry**. It is ministry uncontaminated by the kind of concern about self that creeps in and takes over like an invasive plant in your garden. It is ministry unmarred by the focus on self that dulls our awareness of what others are going through, that confuses our messages and contorts the signals we give to others, and that overrides our courage.

The heart of my workshops focuses on the Three Principles of Excellence. These will be explained in the chapters ahead and might also be called the Three Principles of Health, because these same three principles contribute to high levels of both health and excellence. Emerging from my observations of pastors and candidates, plus the bishop's idea to look to his best pastors, I have concluded that anyone can adopt the Three Principles. Anyone can start on the journey toward excellence in ministry by simply deciding to. No special talent or even special effort is required to get started, just some changes in thinking. Furthermore, having witnessed some unbelievable mistakes in ministry (no, I am not going to write a sequel called "Sickness and Stupidity in Ministry"!), and having heard of countless heart-wrenching tragedies, I cannot think of a single one that would not have been prevented had the Three Principles been followed. Finally, the Three Principles are the foundation from which everything else follows. I cannot imagine anything excellent happening in ministry that doesn't flow out of the Three Principles.

A Word about Change

Before going on, I want to discuss change. Another denominational official, whom I deeply respect, once told me that what we need in candidates for ministry are people who have the rare gift of being change agents—people who can actually create change and not just talk about it. She was right! Any move toward excellence involves changing ourselves—first upsetting and then rearranging our habits, thus creating something new and better. If we can't change ourselves, how can we ever be change agents in our communities?

Why is change so difficult? Why do churches and pastors return to the same mistakes time after time? Well, listen to what people say when they have just been through a painful experience: "That's over and done with. There's nothing else we could have done then, and nothing we can do about it now." But there is **always** something else, something better we could have done, and if we don't want to face it and admit it because we are too afraid of the guilt we might feel if we did, we are doomed to repeat our mistakes. Our behaviors get repeated not so much because they worked the first time but because it takes energy to change, to stir up what is already comfortably in place. But if we don't change, we become predictable, and predictability takes away any possibility of leadership. What kind of leader are you if you only do what people expect?

Unpredictability and surprise are important, if often over-looked, aspects of good leadership—**judicious** surprise, mind you! Pursuing excellence involves staying aware that as we choose to do what we do, we'll discover a vast world of possibilities. The key is not to let the past determine your choices in the present, not to follow those who say, "But we've always done it this way." Become a leader of yourself, a change agent, an unpredictable and continuous seeker of excellence.

Enough pep talk. Below is the first in a series of exercises I offer at the end of each chapter to make the experience of reading this book as much like attending one of my workshops as possible. In other words, if you engage with the exercises, you are much more likely to be a participant, as opposed to a casual observer, on the road to health and excellence in ministry.

Exercise

Take a few moments at the beginning of a work day, or just before going into an important encounter or meeting, and search your awareness for anything like "self-concern." In your journal, list the self-concern items you discover. In whatever manner you can, attempt to put those concerns on hold—out of your awareness—and proceed without them. At the end of your day, or soon after that important encounter or meeting, revisit your list of self-concerns and describe your means of attempting to put them out of your awareness, comment on the effectiveness of your attempt, and finally journal your thoughts about the impact this exercise had on your participation and effectiveness in your ministry.

CHAPTER 2
Our Season of Disrespect
Not So Great Expectations

What makes the exploits of my highest performing clients especially remarkable is that they took place during our long season of disrespect. Since I first began working at the Midwest Ministry Development Center in 1970 to the present, the profession of ministry has been in a struggle for respect. We have seen bright moments in the history of the last thirty years when that struggle has eased, but the struggle itself and its consequences have been with us throughout.

Ironically, I owe much to that struggle. These development centers (of which there are now seven, operating in eleven locations) originated in the late 1960s. Denominational officials were noting that an alarming number of highly talented clergy were leaving the ranks. The centers, called Career Development Centers at the time, were established in order to stem that flow. The thought was to offer individuals a way to plan for longevity in their ministry careers by matching their gifts and dreams with possibilities. We suspected that many were leaving because of the notion that they could find more productive ways of changing the world than staying in ministry. Such was the state of our disrespect.

A bright moment occurred shortly after I started working at the Midwest Ministry Development Center. By the mid-1970s, women began entering the professional ministry in increasing numbers. They brought with them a new life, a new spirit, and considerable talent. One of my roles at the center was research, and the research I did at the time convinced me of this: women were raising the bar in ministry with respect to emotional strength and energy. Blessed were the churches who recognized this. But they were scarce in the beginning. I recall one denominational executive reporting his tears of joy when he went to help a congregation in their search for a new pastor and they told him, "All things being equal, we would like our next pastor to be a woman."

By the 1980s, headlines began chronicling sexual misconduct among the clergy, and the smoldering sparks of public disrespect for the profession began to blaze again. When the abuse involved children and adolescents, the outrage, which was of course completely justified, further tainted the profession. The public might have exempted ministers as a whole, since the abusers themselves represented only a tiny fraction. However, a number of clergy in high places, who might well be expected to represent the highest moral and spiritual fiber of the church, were implicated for their roles in covering up and seemingly minimizing the sexual abuse.

However, in recent years, another bright light has been shining as churches are reaching out with creative forms of worship and evangelism to draw in many who previously would have never set foot in a church. And it must be added that throughout this extended period of disrespect, there have been countless acts of faithful ministry, and even heroism, in churches large and small, on mission fields, schools, street corners, hospitals, prisons, and battlefields. These have not gone unnoticed. But ministers are not granted automatic respect as they may have been in the past. In the past, their presence was honored, their words clung to, their authority from God taken for granted. Not many would have dared to say, "I don't agree with what she is doing" or "it's time for him to move on."

The negative consequences of this struggle over the respect for clergy have been many. One consequence has been in the selection/recruitment process. We will never know how many gifted individuals have avoided ministry because of the culture of disrespect toward it.[1] Among those who have been in the profession, the sting of disrespect has hurt some much more than others. But my clients who excel in ministry seemingly have ignored it, perhaps as a matter of self-concern that had no place in their work. They are among the stalwarts who probably say, "So what! Jesus never said 'blessed are the respected.'"

Clergy continue to abuse power, and the scandals continue to shock us. Only now the signs of this disrespect are more internal than external or explicit. In fact, if I went into most church communities and inquired about the pastor, I would probably not hear overt disrespect in return. I would hear: "He's so kind to our elderly." "She was such a comfort when my mother died." "He's such a good role model for our young people." "She makes the Bible come alive in her teaching and preaching." Such testimonies collectively speak well of pastors meeting expectations and maintaining the status quo, but not of courageous, difference-making ministry. If pastors are to earn true respect, it will be through impactful ministry leadership that enables individuals and organizations to move to higher levels of health and effectiveness.

The natural response when you long for respect is to try to please others, and the result of too much trying to please others when you are in ministry is that you lose your way. You come to the point of feeling like you are not your own person. You end up not valuing what you are doing but for many reasons feeling stuck in it. Depression often sets in.

Initiative all but disappears when you are busy fearing loss of respect. The time spent in ministry can be divided into three categories: responding, maintaining, and initiating. Most pastoral care comes under the heading of responding. Maintaining includes a lot of odds and ends such as proofreading the Sunday bulletin, committee meetings, and staff supervision. Initiating is where vision and courage come into play. All three modes are important, and the percentages of time you will spend in each will depend on the type of ministry you are in, but I am convinced that when the percentage of time spent initiating in ministry drops below a certain level, the possibility of depression increases. You start losing touch with the idealism that got you into ministry in the first place. You allow the heart of the most meaningful part of your calling to slip away.

So what do we do? There is one particular symptom—and result—of the disrespect that I believe is very much worth considering. It is one that strongly suggests a way out. It is this: *we do not expect nearly enough of people in ministry. Those of us in ministry do not expect enough of ourselves.* And those not-so-great expectations do ministry a great disservice. Lack of respect for clergy lowers expectations, and lowered expectations fosters ministry malaise. Pastors can be very busy, but high expectations have nothing to do with being busy. We need to rethink what we mean by "expectations" and discover afresh how having genuinely high expectations links integrally with health and happiness in ministry.

To illustrate the point, a hundred stories I have heard can be condensed into one. Let's say that Pastor Smith is called to a new parish and "enjoys" a honeymoon period (when he can do no wrong) that lasts anywhere from twenty minutes to two years. (The twenty-minute honeymoon actually did occur and is described in Chapter 3.) However long it is, during that honeymoon period pressure builds in the form of withheld criticisms of Pastor Smith. At the end of the honeymoon, the pressure valve is opened, usually slowly, and the critiques begin to leak out. When the pastor becomes aware of the first criticisms, he does the natural, but not the excellent, thing. He avoids the critics. Eventually the critics in exasperation take their complaints to the bishop (or the equivalent). The bishop calls Pastor Smith in for a chat and finds it in her best interest (she is swamped with other concerns) to believe Pastor Smith's explanation that the criticism is petty, comes from a handful of insignificant ne'er-do-wells, and that everything is under control. Pressure continues to build, however, and the bishop is alerted a second time. Awakened, the bishop appoints a team to go in and investigate.

From that point on, I have never heard that it has gone well for Pastor Smith. The outside committee takes over, interviewing as many of the involved critics as possible, drawing conclusions, and making recommendations. Pastor Smith has, in effect, been pushed aside. The implication is that the pastor is a failure—and the committee had to "fix it" for him. Pastor Smith ends up slinking to another congregation and starting ministry there as a fearful, unconfident, and angry person (who hasn't stopped brooding over the termination package). What about expectations? It would be far better if the bishop, church moderator, or executive minister had said, "Pastor, you were part of creating this mess. You figure out what to do and lead this church out of it. I'm here to support you in that task." In this scenario, whether the pastor stays or leaves, the church witnesses a leader who has seen to it that the best outcome occurs. The church benefits and the pastor moves forward as a person of integrity. Excellent ministry often takes the form of a two-step process. Step one: you create trouble, sometimes intentionally and sometimes unintentionally. Step two: you take the broken pieces and make something positive out of them. Far too many ministers follow a career path of completing step one and then moving on.

What if pastors expected more of themselves? By "expecting more of themselves," I don't mean beating their heads against a brick wall by working longer hours. Instead, I mean expecting to lead an effective and well-balanced life of ministry. Having a rich personal life of *health* will be essential to sustaining the *excellence* of your ministry. If you follow the Three Principles of Health and Excellence in the chapters ahead, work will become lighter and much more meaningful. And, if you follow the Rules of Strength in Chapter 12, you will never beat your head against a brick wall again. Guaranteed!

You will also gain that missing commodity, respect, from your people and among your ministry peers. The key is found in an important term that you will hear frequently as we continue. The term is *intentions*. If you intentionally set your expectations of yourself higher and communicate them to others, people will respect you for it. Of course, they will also expect you to live up to your intentions. But that is no more than you are expecting of yourself! I have firmly come to believe in the saying that *you get what you expect*. Watching my clients at the Center has totally convinced me of that. Therefore, be both thoughtful and generous with your intentions. They have a lot of power to lead you toward or away from both health and excellence, as you'll see in more detail in Chapter 8.

Exercise

Write a list of five things you do in your work under each of these two headings: (1) Things I do that contribute significantly to my sense of professional meaning and self-respect; (2) Things I do that add nothing to or detract from my professional meaning and self-respect. Then take each item from your second list and make a statement about (a) how you could eliminate that activity from your agenda, or (b) how you could make it a more positive experience for yourself.

Note
1. Gallup reports a decline from 1985, when 67 percent of the general public had a "high or very high" level of respect for the honesty and ethics of clergy, to a new low of 37 percent in 2018. To compare to other professions, see https://news.gallup.com/poll/245597/nurses-again-outpace-professions-honesty-ethics.aspx.

CHAPTER 3

The Lesson from the Twenty-Minute Honeymoon

In Chapter 2, I mentioned in passing the twenty-minute honeymoon. Allow me to explain. Andrea's bishop sent her to me. The bishop's referral plea was almost as short as: "What can I do with her?" Andrea was a woman in her mid-twenties who had been called to a congregation to be their youth pastor. She was not the least hesitant to talk about her twenty-minute honeymoon. On her first Sunday and twenty minutes into the service, she had gathered the children around her at the front of the church and was engaging them in the "children's moment." In the midst of her discourse with them, she used the term "pissed off." Taking seriously their role as protectors of young ears, the powers-that-be in the church scrambled to call a meeting immediately following the service. They called Andrea in and fired her.

Why had she used that phrase in a children's talk? Andrea told me that it was because she felt so good, so comfortable in the moment. It just came out! I reinterpreted her take on the situation from "comfort" to "non-anxious presence run amok." While feeling connected to the children, she had forgotten the appropriate care and self-monitoring that every professional needs to maintain.

The story has a happy ending. With Andrea's permission, I later called the bishop and said, "By all means, find her another church. She has learned her lesson. She is good! The church will get the most effective and talented youth minister they could hope for."

The bishop, somewhat to my surprise, was pleased. That's exactly the impression he had of her.

Honeymoons

Beware of the honeymoons that pastors supposedly get to enjoy! Honeymoons are misleading. A honeymoon is a time of euphoria and lack of realism, a time that cannot last. Andrea's case being an exception, the honeymoon is the time when what you do that rankles or offends is never mentioned to you. It is human nature to interpret silence as approval, so you keep on rankling and offending. And sooner or later, the honeymoon ends and reality dawns. Smoldering resentment is not fertile ground for good pastoral rapport.

The comfort of the honeymoon can be misleading, as Andrea would attest. Comfort is part of your self-care, but in a very important sense, it is not a part of your excellence. Often we face the choice of being either a seeker of comfort or a seeker of truth. Athletes or performers, for example, do not improve by seeking comfort. Rather, they seek challenges on which they can act. You may face challenges in bringing difficult content into your sermon, content that might stir up discomfort for you and your congregation. The issue of comfort comes up every time you have a difficult decision to make, and the choice is always between comfortable stagnation or challenging growth. Our instinct is often to sidestep conflict or tension points, thinking it is safer. But truly excellent ministry involves moving toward those difficulties and embracing them as the "stuff of ministry," the "stuff of life."

There are too many individually unique and intervening circumstances for anyone to say that you *always* have to choose to move away from comfort. But know that the more you take yourself toward challenges, the farther down the road to excellence you will go. Regarding excellence, *discomfort* is often your friend. The nagging, uncomfortable feeling that something is not right is often your only protection against doing something disastrous. Value that sensitivity; never ignore it.

Initiative

It is challenging to develop the initiative required in leadership to change things for the better. Initiative means plunging into the unknown, and that brings about discomfort. To accept and deal with discomfort requires courage. Paradoxically, when you act as courageously as you can in persevering through discomfort, only then do you reach the epitome of comfort, the comfort of knowing that what you did was right as well as excellent.

This sort of comfort is hard won by persevering through discomfort. Compare this hard-won comfort to a time when perhaps, instead of acting at the right moment to confront a conflict, you retreated to the comfort of your study to polish the sermon you had finished writing two days earlier. Nobody noticed the difference, but the comfort you sought ended up being a jagged, troubled, and fragmented comfort. When the chips are down, most choices for comfort end up that way. But the jagged, troubled, fragmented part of discomfort is actually your friend.

The fact is that troubled waters are always there. If you look about your community, then your church, and then your own family, you will note more troubled waters than you can deal with! You could start at many different places, but at the end of the day you have to start somewhere. That's all you can do.

The following exercise is one of my favorites. I invite my clients to spend a period of time identifying (usually writing down) as many examples of troubled waters in their lives as they can recall, including in their community, church, and family. The examples that clients provide can be revelatory. Then I ask them to write a courage list—not a list of things they *will* do, but a list of things that, using their imagination, *would be possible* for someone with unlimited courage to do. The instructions include naming courageous possibilities that would address the troubled waters. At a minimum, what happens is that doing this exercise changes the leaders' outlook. They see their ministries differently. They brighten, and they "lean in," as if ready to go. They see themselves differently with the realization that "maybe I could," "maybe I do have that courage in me." And when I sneakily ask, "Which one will you tackle first?" they respond without breaking stride, as if they knew all along they were about to change.

Exercise

Write down five examples of troubled waters currently existing in your community, church, or home. Choose one of those examples and write a "courage list" in relation to it. According to the rules of the courage list, focus (at least for now) not on the question "What will I do?" Instead, ask yourself, "What would be the most courageous steps I could take if I had unlimited courage?"

Extra Credit: Choose one of those courageous steps and do it!

CHAPTER 4

Preparation for the Journey

Pursuing authentic excellence in ministry is a journey. Before going further, however, I want us to spend some time with three items that are important for the trip ahead. Two are terms that need defining; the third is someone I want you to meet.

Depths

The first term is *depths,* a critically important concept for what lies ahead. I am convinced that all excellence in ministry comes from our depths, and it is there that we come to understand the key to health. I began to use the term *depths* long before I tried to define it. I routinely asked clients, "What do you find when you go into your depths?" I eventually found it to be my favorite question. At times the blank look on someone's face caused me to wonder if I might be inquiring about something that was a figment of my imagination. What are "depths" anyway? But when I asked the question of my sharpest clients, they had no hesitation before responding, and they responded as if "the depths" was a place they visited often. Furthermore, I found an amazing consistency in what they reported finding there. I knew then that whatever it was, it was real.

But I eventually decided that I had better give *depths* a definition. I knew for certain it is not geographical, like an underground cave. I also knew it is not anatomical, like a place in the pit of our stomach (though that imagery might help us get there). I finally decided that it is a state of mind, a state of acute awareness, a state in which we remove ourselves far enough from the ordinary trivialities and desperations that fill our everyday lives so as to see and understand things that we ordinarily don't. Deep enough into our depths we find God, or God finds us—it doesn't seem to matter which. My best clients report finding peace when they go to their depths.

Depths is a relative term. One person's depths will be deeper than another's. We all have different ways of accessing those depths as well. A work of art, a meaningful piece of music, a Scripture passage that has a special resonance for us, twenty minutes of quiet meditation—many doors can open us to our depths. Practicing a sabbath (whether one day a week, one hour a day, or another rhythm) is a long-proven spiritual door that pastors are prone to neglect. The point is to use the door that works for you and to become well-acquainted with the reality that will meet you at that deep point. To whatever degree we can enter into our own depths, we come closer to seeing what we need to see and feeling what we need to feel in order to behave in truly excellent ways.

Operational Belief

The second term that needs to be defined at this point is quite different. It is *operational belief.* An *operational belief* is one that we adopt for a positive purpose, not because we absolutely know that it is true but because we know what it will enable us to do. We act on it and communicate as if it were true—all for a loving purpose. We will come across many examples of operational beliefs in the chapters to come. What happens frequently is that we start by acting out the belief, and at some point we realize it has become a genuine belief, one that we experience as true.

An example is the deliberate adoption of the following belief: Since we are all created uniquely, there is a unique spark of genius in everyone. If we decide to find that spark in everyone we encounter, those encounters are likely to undergo a subtle change

21

that may have a very positive impact. Additionally, we might think about the belief that "you can do anything you set your mind to." Of course, this is not entirely true. However, this operational belief helps us approach our tasks with a sense of optimism and enthusiasm that can lead to success. It is well known that teachers who have been told that their students are special achievers will treat their students in a way that helps them to actually become special achievers, while those who have been told that their students are below par have the opposite effect. We can choose to have operational beliefs that line up with our theological belief that God is active in the world.

Meet Your Coach

I told you I wanted to introduce you to someone. This is someone you will find to be indispensable as you take this journey. Meet your coach. You absolutely need a coach! Before you start envisioning dollar signs flying away from you like a flock of frightened birds, let me assure you that this coach will fit nicely into your budget. You can, and should, be *your own coach*. A coach is someone who can observe you and give you critical feedback for improvement, as well as the motivation you need to accomplish your goals. A coach is not immersed in the immediate struggles of one's life but one step removed—close enough to be connected, but far enough back to bring in fresh perspectives and new options of thinking and behavior. I know of some very good coaches who work with clergy, and they are worth every penny. But the ultimate goal of any coach should be that you develop your own ability to coach yourself. On this journey, you are to embark on developing your own inner coach. You are to develop skills such that you can be self-critical and motivated, which will help you achieve excellence. Consider this book to be a training manual for your inner coach.

You have the technical wiring in place already: you talk to yourself! Everybody does. Only the messages usually run something like: "You stupid idiot, you never do anything right" (the "incompetent" message) and "Nothing ever goes right for me" (the "victim" message). You may have internalized the first message, that of incompetency, by hearing it from your parents or teachers or other adults in your life, frustrated as they were, more than once, by your behavior. You could have picked up the second message anywhere—peers, spouse, colleagues. The victim message is so prevalent. The first step is to confront and erase those messages. Then you reprogram your coach with a whole new set.

In addition to those two inner messages mentioned above, you also have other conversations with yourself—inner debates about whether you should do this or that. You might as well give one of those voices a constant personality and purpose. Sometimes you will say, "I don't feel like going to troubled waters today." Your coach has been trained to say, "But isn't that who you say you want to be?" If that seems a little overbearing to you, remember that good coaches don't have fits when you don't listen to them. They are patient. And you want a good coach. A good coach believes in you and encourages you when things aren't going so well. But a good coach is also tough, and in the long run does what needs to be done to keep you on track. A good coach keeps you focused on the most important things. Your inner coach will be with you twenty-four hours a day, and I am completely serious when I say that your sense of loneliness will be cut to almost nothing.

I have a vision of you and your inner coach. It is like a split-screen television image. On one side of the screen, you are in the midst of a whirlwind of chaos, with comments and heated discussions flying all over the place (like some church council meetings!). On the other side of the screen, your coach is in your depths, remaining calm in the midst of chaos and confusion. The communication between you and your coach is clear and gives you a perspective and assurance that is confident about what to do. You combine the universe-scoping wisdom of an ascetic monk with the adrenalin supercharge of a galloping rescuer, and the troubled waters are stilled by your valiant and sage leadership. It's a kind of episodic version of "in this world but not of this world."

Now that I have introduced you, I hope that you will become the best the of friends!

Exercise

Think of at least two of your operational beliefs (beliefs you've adopted because they aid you in accomplishing a good purpose). Write them down and reflect on how you have come to trust them and count them as true. Then construct two more operational beliefs that would be new to you and beneficial to your ministry. (It will be interesting to compare these with examples you will encounter later in this book.)

PART 2

Health

CHAPTER 5

An Overview of Health in Ministry

Why should we be especially concerned about health when we are looking at excellence in ministry? What is the connection between the two? Is health in ministry different from health anywhere else?

We can begin by saying that everything we do is dependent on our health. The kind of ministry that shuns comfort and embraces courage also requires certain strengths, the cultivation of which would fall under what we call "health." Clearly those strengths go beyond the mere absence of symptoms. We can define physical health using charts and tables and checklists used in annual wellness exams. Mental health can be defined by the absence of dysfunctions categorized in the *Diagnostic and Statistical Manual of Mental Disorders*. But we need to go beyond the standard definitions when it comes to health in ministry. What lies beyond is very difficult to define, however. We can use words such as *vibrant, glowing, vigorous, buoyant,* and *exuberant,* but what do such words really tell us, and how do they apply to ministry?

Let's start at the other end with the question: "What is required for high-quality ministry?" Health, of course, is one of the elements required. Certain states of mind, or attitudes, are part of what goes beyond the normal definition of health. Ultimately, it is impossible to come up with new models that include *all* the relevant data that go beyond normal conceptions of health. To put it another way, there is no way we could come up with an adequate health meter that would serve our purposes. The reason is simple: Our God-given capacity for health contains regions we have barely begun to explore. One evident feature of that capacity is summed up by the words *flexible, adaptive,* and *compensatory.* I have known many people, including one of my brightest and best clients, who from birth have suffered physical infirmities that I would have found unbearable, yet who, by virtue of incredible attitude, would score very high on our imaginary health meter. I could name a roomful of ministers with bipolar disorder—a condition that is potentially ruinous to health—who, through a healthy attitude and faithful adherence to a medication regimen, offer high-quality ministry and exhibit strong overall health. The good news is that almost no condition excludes you from some measure of health in ministry.

I see two directions in which to approach the connection between health and excellence in ministry. The direction taken throughout most of this book is what health can do for excellence in ministry. In recent history, the major concern has come from the opposite direction, that of how the way we are doing ministry is affecting our health. As you may remember, in the mid-1980s a wave of concern arose about health issues in ministry. Whenever you saw the word *clergy* in print, more often than not it was accompanied by another term, *burnout.* Clergy burnout was apparently rampant, and it encompassed a range of ills including exhaustion, depression, alcohol abuse, sexual misconduct, and, in extreme cases, death on the job. Every other minister seemed to be on the verge of burnout—if they weren't burnt out already.

Health and life insurance companies specializing in working with clergy and their families took notice, and with their vested interest they sponsored several conferences to explore the issue and generate some initiatives to reverse the trend. A discussion group at one of those conferences I attended painted a frightening but accurate picture: *the pastor working himself or herself half to death trying to beat life back into a sick and dying congregation.* The irony, of course, is that the state of health of the congregation takes its lead from the state of health of the pastor and pastoral staff.

A Tale of Two Bullies

Let's look further at this symbiotic relationship between the health of the pastor and the health of the congregation. If you are not convinced you should care about your health for your own sake, maybe you will for the sake of your congregation. Rather than spending time discussing the theory or dynamics of why this happens, I will tell you a story. It's a composite of many true stories I have heard over the years. It features two main characters: Pastor Blue, a beleaguered, depressed cleric; and Conrad Troll, a major influencer behind everything done at the church. I entitle my story "The Tale of Two Bullies."

Let's start with Pastor Blue, a candidate for burnout. The main culprit behind Pastor Blue's descent into miserable health is his life-long companion, bully number one: *Guilt*. Guilt, whether creeping in softly or charging in, is the motivation behind everything Pastor Blue does in ministry. All of his pastoral work amounts to meeting obligations he believes he owes in order to make up for his insufficiencies. He is on his shakiest ground when he tries to preach about forgiveness because has never had any personal experience of it. When you act out of guilt, you never act wholeheartedly. You generally are at some level of war within yourself, with resentment fighting against what you are doing. The resentment comes from deep down, not wanting to do whatever obligation that guilt is compelling you to do. Even though the war is usually unconscious, over time it takes a major toll on your health, both physical and emotional. And what people get from you is less than inspiring. At his very best, Pastor Blue's sermons fail to reach the level of preaching the Good News and come through as proclaiming the "somewhat above-average news" of the gospel.

This does not mean that things come to a standstill at the church. Some people still come, and some people are willing to fill the spots on committees. Who are those people? They are those who are also inclined to feel guilty, of course. Pastor Blue has used the only thing he knows about motivation (it starts with a *g*), and the natural process of selection—selection of those most susceptible to guilt—occurs. The work done by the laity is done by those who share the same ambivalence and ultimately the same resentment.

At this point in the story, let's skip to Conrad Troll, bully number two. He alone looks at Pastor Blue and is thrilled. Here is someone he knows he can control. Very familiar with guilt himself, he sees clearly that he can easily play on Pastor Blue's need to work out his guilt, and he does. This is no different from how he relates to the rest of the church. He has a knack for getting people to agree with him, or to get them out of the way. He is too smart to use obvious intimidation. He knows how to make people feel guilty if they do not agree with him. So he runs virtually everything, especially Pastor Blue. Pastor Blue, in turn, has begun to suffer from a haunting feeling that he is not his own person and does not have control over his own ministry. He does not know why but is certain that the remedy is to work harder and for longer hours, which is just how Conrad likes it.

At the end of Pastor Blue's workday, he realizes it's time to go home. But the work is not finished (it never is). He knows his family is expecting him for dinner, so he goes home—but feels guilty for doing so. At home, he isn't really there. All evening long his thoughts are pulled back to the church, the people unvisited, the crises unattended, the sermon not finished. He is not emotionally or mentally available to his wife and children. And he definitely is not there for himself. Perhaps what he needs most for the sake of his health is a hug, an affirmation, a moment of joy, or even an hour of rest. But those things could not be further from his mind, and the way he acts does not invite affection or support from his family, who should be the ones to supply such affirmation. Maybe for one evening this doesn't matter. But for

Pastor Blue these evenings repeat themselves over and over again. He robs himself of a personal life, and after a while he has nothing by way of personal experience to share. He has nothing to say that is authentic. Taking their cue from the way the pastor talks, the people of the congregation, while at church, begin to talk only of things that are not real to them. Pastor Blue's unhealthiness now infects the church.

Because of guilt, Pastor Blue has a hard time leaving work behind. It is the height of arrogance to think that the sky will fall if you are not ministering, or even available to minister, to the world twenty-four hours a day. It may be too much to expect that the minute you leave work, you will totally forget you are a minister. But I would encourage you to at least make that your aim. Your family will thank you!

Now let me introduce you to Brian. Even though he is the senior pastor of a large metropolitan congregation, Brian leaves his work behind when he goes off duty—and that is a good thing! That is why he is near the top of the list of my best and brightest clients. Because Brian knows how to separate his work and leisure, he has one of the most fulfilling personal lives of anyone I know. Many of the things that are on my bucket list Brian has already done. Does he act like a wild and woolly outlaw on his own time? Absolutely not! If you can stay on the straight and narrow ethically and morally only by reminding yourself that you are a minister, it's time to take a close look at your character.

Brian's rich personal life feeds his ministry in countless ways, starting with the easy, warm smile on his face. It doesn't hurt, either, that talking with him is always very interesting. I could point to many ways in which Brian shows excellent leadership, but I will settle on one. The relationship he has with his large staff—the respect, support, and loving attention he gives them— almost brings tears to my eyes. It is to his credit that at least two of his staff are also among my top clients. Brian shows an immediate, unmistakable, unhurried care for others that is supported by his unstinting care for himself. He is a walking demonstration of the reciprocal bond between health and excellence.

Exercise

Before finishing your work for the day and leaving for home, focus on leaving behind the concerns that will detract from the time ahead, which has potential for personal restoration, positive opportunities with family and/or friends, and creative self-expression. Identify what things you'd like to leave behind and describe your attempt to set them aside. Then journal about that process—how you went about it and how you felt about it. Later, at the end of the day, write down your impressions and how your transition time impacted the rest of the day.

CHAPTER 6

Self-Care vs. Self-Concern

I have mentioned self-concern throughout much of this book so far and have cited many examples. Still, it has been my experience that, in my workshops, confusion arises over the difference between self-concern and self-care. They sound similar. They are in many ways opposites; they are also related. Self-care can be divided into four branches, and we will look briefly at each of the four in this chapter.

Self-Concern

One of the branches of self-care is self-concern. Self-concern in and of itself is not inherently bad. We all experience it. Self-concern is not selfishness. The point at which it becomes damaging to our health is when we don't do anything about it, when it lingers and becomes worry, when it becomes stuck. Then it is like an acid that eats away at our health. Self-concern becomes damaging to our ministry when it distracts us from attending to what we are called to do. It is also damaging to our ministry when it contaminates our motives—when we pretend to be caring for others but we are actually taking care of ourselves. Avoiding conflict, for example, is more about self-concern than it is about effectively resolving conflict in the church. It is damaging to our ministries when it prevents us from going into our depths.

I have often heard pastors talk about being worried about one of their children, most often a young adult who appears to be "lost." In our discussion, this goes under the heading of self-concern even though it is concern for another, because it has the same impact on one's ministry. Any self-concern can distract the pastor from focusing exclusively on ministry. It inevitably does. The self-care response begins with the Serenity Prayer:

> God, grant me the serenity to accept the things I cannot change, Courage to change the things I can, And wisdom to know the difference.

At this point in working with the worried parent (because he or she is in the parent role, not the pastor role), I invoke the importance of self-care: "You must do something active about this worry, for your sake, for your ministry's sake, and for your child's sake, and then let it go." We then work together to figure out a plan that the parent can use to cope with the stress of worrying and that will have a helpful impact on the situation. Whatever is decided must be done. I almost always suggest the operational belief that leads to the parent saying to the child: "I believe in you and trust that you will find your way, the way that will be best for you. I care about you and am willing to help in any way you ask me to. In the meantime, I leave it in your capable hands, and God's." Sometimes that statement is all you can do, but at the same time it may count for a lot. It may empower your child to believe in himself or herself, and it may empower you to let go.

One other prevalent manifestation of self-concern is worry about time. We are anxious over never having enough time, and so we rush and stew—the former hurting our work and the latter damaging our health. We miss the eternal moment. The present is the only real "space" that we live in, and we vacate that space when we try to rush through it or focus on all we have to get done by some future deadline.

What does self-care bring to this problem? For starters, self-care through your coach (see Chapter 4) tells you: "Do less and do it better." Plan bigger chunks of time for each thing you do, and take on far fewer tasks. The problem here has to do with commitment. Be very careful what you commit yourself to. The problem with most clergy is that they feel obligated to say yes to every request. They have this belief that God never says no (that's a joke!) and that they should not either. The inevitable result is that they load themselves up with totally unrealistic expectations of the quantity of the work they intend to get done, without considering the toll it will take on quality. They zoom through the items on their "must do" list, lest they let people down. Yet more than once I have heard people say, "Don't count on the pastor. He's so busy, he won't get around to it." Taking a look at one's unrealistic expectations and difficulty saying "no" is key to finding personal and professional health and excellence.

Let's look now at the other three branches of self-care, which I call *practices, boundaries,* and *monitoring.* In other words, what you do, what you don't do, and what you pay attention to.

Practices

We won't spend much time here. Practices include many things that are commonplace, like brushing your teeth twice a day, having an annual wellness exam, and exercising regularly. Other practices may include doing the most difficult but distasteful things as early in the day as possible. That way you will not have to spend your day nervously fretting; you can spend it, instead, feeling good about what you have already accomplished. You and your inner coach can come up with dozens of these tasks. Of course, this presupposes that you have learned about, and you live by, prioritizing these practices. The following chapter will deal more specifically with healthy practices.

Boundaries

Boundaries are simply the things that you *won't* do. Simple or not, boundaries are indispensable to self-care. Your boundaries are in many ways the best part of you. They define your character; they are what make you a safe person for others. Nevertheless, when denominations began to require that their pastors attend boundary training, many ministers found it to be of little value. Boundaries were often presented as a set of prohibitions that seemed arbitrary and alienating, rather than as a constructive, healthy way to connect with people in ministry.

I knew this perspective on boundaries was wrong. I was fortunate to have my first conscious experience of setting healthy boundaries be a positive one. It's a story I love to tell. Early in high school, I had a friend whom I admired. Dick was always a better athlete than I was. One Fourth of July, Dick and I and some of our buddies were attending a celebration at the University of Illinois football stadium. We looked over a couple of rows and saw a guy that looked weird to us. We started to laugh and make jokes—all of us, that is, except Dick. He stopped us and said, "Guys, I looked at myself in the mirror the other day (Dick was better looking than me) and decided that never in my life will I ever make fun of how someone else looks." I was stunned. After a brief moment of feeling ashamed, I was overcome by another feeling, a powerful kind of admiration and respect that I had never known before. I said to myself, "Oh, that's the way to be. That's how *I* want to be!"

Boundaries are like that: clarity about who one is and who one intends to be contributes to healthy boundaries. In the movie *Moonstruck*, the character played by Olympia Dukakis was asked by a male friend, "Why don't you have an affair like your husband is doing?" Her reply was simply, "I don't have to. I know who I am."

If you are clear about your boundaries, you know yourself in a way that honors your health. Your boundaries are *yours*. They are one category of things about yourself that you create. Others might try to impose some on you, but they are not part of your health until you say, "This is the way to be. This is how *I* want to be."

Boundaries are a way of caring for yourself. Of obvious importance are your boundaries that say: "I will not knowingly take into my body anything that will harm it." Going further, I hope you have a boundary that says: "I will not, except under extreme circumstances of being called to save someone else's life, do anything that will risk serious injury or death to myself." Some boundaries can help you avoid depression, such as: "I will not allow myself to become so invested in any outcome that I would become depressed if I don't get my way." (As a Cubs fan, I learned that one early.)

One of the important benefits about setting clear boundaries is that they become automatic. It's a good idea to think about them every once in a while—to review them, feel good about them, and reinforce them. It is also important to tell others what your boundaries are, so that they know they can trust you. But when the chips are down and it's time to apply your boundaries, you don't have to take time to stop and think. You know who you are, and others know who you are, too!

Monitoring

The monitoring that is important to self-care is a special kind of "listening." (Listening is in quotes out of respect for the hearing impaired, who have their own way of covering this function.) The listening I'm referring to is one that the hearing-impaired do exactly the same way as everyone else. It is listening to some inner voices—three, to be exact. I started out in my first workshops talking about this, and then almost gave it up. I figured you could only push people so far into talking to themselves. Then, when one person told me this was the most helpful thing she got from the workshop, I decided to keep it.

Consider that you have three inner voices: one is a voice for the body; the second is a voice for your spirit or mood; the third is a voice for your agenda or intentions. It is very important that they talk to each other. Rather than going into how that works, let's "listen" in on a typical conversation.

> AGENDA: I think it's important that we stay up a little longer and finish this sermon.

> BODY: Oh, come on, Agenda! It's past midnight and it's been a rough day. I need my sleep!

> AGENDA: I know that, Body, but this is *really* important. I'll tell you what: if you will go along with me this time, I promise you that I'll make it up to you tomorrow. You can sleep in until eight o'clock, and in the afternoon I'll buy you that hot fudge sundae you've been craving.

> BODY: Hot fudge, huh? Throw in a visit to the gym in the evening, and you've got a deal.

> AGENDA: Agreed! Okay, that's settled. Now let's move ahead.

> SPIRIT: Wait a minute! I'm bored out of my gourd with this sermon. If we're going to say something, I want it to be something worthwhile.

Later, as I interviewed Agenda about this exchange, here is what I heard Agenda saying:

It was really important that we had that conversation. I know if we don't talk regularly, I tend to run roughshod over Body and Spirit. If Body isn't listened to, it can get really nasty. I sometimes think Body could qualify as having a passive-aggressive personality disorder. And as for Spirit—if Spirit was bored, can you imagine how the congregation felt? We had to stay up a little longer to fix that sermon, and I had to up the hot fudge sundae to a banana split to ward off another protest from Body. But in the end, it was worth it.

I think you get the idea.

Exercise

Write out a list of your *practices* (things you regularly do for self-care) and *boundaries* (things that, for the sake of self-care, you will not do). Imagine that you are an impartial observer following yourself around for a week, and then being asked to describe how you relate to your family, to your congregation, to your staff, and so on. Then write out a second list of practices and boundaries that would represent your epitome of health in relation to each of these groups. Finally, plan what you can do to close the gap between your actual practices and boundaries and those to which you would aspire.

CHAPTER 7

Health Summarized
Wholeness, Happiness, and Weightlessness

The *Grade Yourself* exercise (found in Appendix A) identifies eleven areas of health and asks you to evaluate how healthy your behavior is in each area. One area in Part I, the Rhythms of Life, relates primarily to physical health (the voice for your body). Five additional areas in Part I relate to needs that you experience (as told to you by the voice for your spirit), and five areas in Part II relate to various relationships (with which your voice for your intentions, your agenda, is concerned). Relationships are included because the notion of health that we are working with goes far beyond your individual health. Your health is tied to the health of your environment and the health of those around you. Attending to your health involves not only looking out for yourself but also attempting to bring wholeness, happiness, and weightlessness (qualities we are about to describe) to others.

I designed *Grade Yourself* for use in workshops as the start of a process. Participants were given only thirty minutes to complete it, so the verbal instructions were not to ponder analytically over each area but to grade yourself according to your quick intuitive sense. Small groups then picked up the process, brainstorming together on how participants could make improvements in the areas that most caught their attention. This proved to work well. As I have said many times, most clergy could write the book on health—even if they don't follow their own advice. At least they can help one another.

This same process suited me just fine. At one point when I was devoting much of my time to health and excellence, I ended up in the hospital twice in one week—the first time for rotator cuff surgery, and the second with a blood clot in my lung. While I was lying there with a big, funny-looking device keeping my shoulder immobilized and tubes coming into my body all over the place, my daughter Susan came to visit me. She took one look and said, "Dad, you had better work hard at this excellence thing, or you're not going to have much credibility talking about health!" She was right. So I let workshop participants help me define the key components of health.

My questionable credibility notwithstanding, I would like to attempt a reasonable summary of health before moving on to excellence. For that purpose, I have chosen the words *wholeness, happiness,* and *weightlessness.*

Wholeness

Wholeness is a useful metaphor for health. Health is generally understood as all the parts of the *whole* body working together. In Chapter 6, we had a brief glimpse of the voices for body, spirit, and intentions, working things out until they were united as a *whole.* A healthy way of conducting yourself in any situation is to take in the *whole* picture of what is going on, decide thoughtfully what to do, and then do it *whole*heartedly. If you are ambivalent or conflicted about what you are about to do, work it out first. A house divided against itself is an unhealthy house. Not much more needs to be said.

Happiness

Happiness is the frosting on the cake of health. No, that's not quite right; it is more than that. Without happiness, health is not health. Consider the following: According to St. Augustine, the only true happiness is found in seeking God. When we do that, we will follow through with God's clear instruction: "Feed my sheep. Love one another." Think about it. Any other attempt to find happiness falls short. If you set out in the morning determined to make yourself happy, it won't happen. If you set out with a healthy intention to make others happy—that's when your own happiness *will* happen. Almost any task—even spearing litter from the roadway, for instance—can be thought of as "loving one another." When you find a person who continually thinks in those terms, you have found a truly happy person—one who is happy because he or she is always looking at the *whole* picture.

Weightlessness

Physical weight is not the focus here. The focus is on the difference between carrying around a sense of heaviness as opposed to a sense of buoyancy about life. Quite often we hear of an important person dying young of a heart attack. In most cases there is a history of *heavy* responsibility implicated in the failure of health. Heavy responsibility—that is, responsibility that feels heavy—is ultimately unhealthy. Being a parent is a big responsibility, to be sure. But big and heavy are not the same. If your responsibility as a parent seems heavy, you are hurting your health, and probably not being the best parent you can be. A shift in attitude is called for, and is well worth the effort. If you can keep your mind on the *whole* picture, even the most frustrating or miserable part of being a parent can be thought of as just a part of something that is joyful, meaningful, and ultimately weightless. The same should be true in ministry: health and excellence are united. So, tell the volunteer lay leaders at your church about weightless responsibility and let them know that this is the only kind of leadership you expect from them. In applying this principle of health to the

41

church, just as you love your child, loving your people, your con-gregation, can lead to ministry that is weightless.

Grade Yourself begins with the rhythms of life. Life, if you haven't noticed, has rhythm. It's a cooperative effort, like writing a piece of music: God provides blank sheet music (our day), and we create the beat and the melody—the repeated daily patterns—that fill it. The day begins with awakening from our dreams (like birth) and ends in our going to sleep (like death). God's part in our day teaches some important lessons.

Just before going to sleep, we are confronted with one, if not the most, important lesson in life, that of *letting go*. We have to let go in order to sleep. We have to let go of our concerns. We have to let go of our conscious thought. But sometimes we have difficul-ty letting go, and we're in for lots of tossing and turning, or even a sleepless night. When it works the way it is supposed to work, the most amazing thing happens. When talking about going to our depths, some will claim that, not being particularly spiritual or contemplative, depths are not something they experience. But that is wrong; every night they have an opportunity to enter their depths when they sleep. And if they are able to let go of control, God will meet them in their depths and bless them with renewal and refreshment.

Sleep is relative; some sleep is better than others. I can tell from my dreams. It is a sign that I haven't let go of control when I have an anxiety dream. It's the dream in which you get up in the pulpit on Sunday morning to preach and suddenly realize you've forgot-ten to prepare a sermon. You awaken relieved that it was only a dream, but some trace of the anxiety stays with you at least until 10 A.M. When we have the other kind of dream, the dream that seems to rise from those "divine depths" within us rather than from our fears and angers, we feel loved. It is not erotic and some-times not even physical, but we know beyond doubt that we have been extravagantly loved. You would think I would be disappointed in waking up and finding it was only a dream. However, the feeling of being loved lasts at least until 10 A.M., and often all day. And thinking about it, I know it wasn't just a dream.

Letting go is the key to weightlessness. Start letting go of some things in life or you're in trouble: your pacifier, your mother's apron strings, many dreams and ambitions, your importance, your awesome tennis serve (personal testimony), and, along the way, many of those whom you love. Letting go is hard, but the failure to do so amounts to health-damaging heaviness.

When I talk about feelings with clients, I usually group feelings into three categories: love, joy, and sorrow. They often wonder why I include sorrow. Sorrow may well be the most important of the three. Sorrow is healing. It is also the *only* doorway to letting go. But sorrow, unlike joy or love, is something that we hope to avoid. Entering sorrow is like the sharp stab of a knife wound, and even if we allow ourselves to get that far, sorrow initially looks like a bottomless pit from which we will never ascend. We find all kinds of ways of avoiding it. The problem is that shutting off sorrow also shuts out both love and joy. We intuitively know that the only way to avoid the pain of sorrow is to have never cared in the first place. And losses that are not let go accumulate and get heavier and heavier.

Guilt that occurs when we break, or are about to break, one of our own boundaries is positive and beneficial to health. It is positive when it pulls us back. But then, when it has done its job, it has to be let go. Forgiveness, which is mentioned more than just in passing in the gospel, *is* letting go. Unfortunately, a great deal of guilt among clergy hangs on and becomes a burden of heaviness. I have encountered many instances of struggle with pornography among clergy, most of it these days via the Internet. Often it develops into a vicious addictive cycle. The individual feels very guilty about the behavior and begins beating himself up internally. After a while he gets fed up with that and seeks relief, which he finds in returning to the behavior that started the guilt. He soon feels even guiltier and the cycle continues, picking up in intensity with each revolution. Once he recognizes the destructiveness he has fallen into, he feels powerless to stop it.

For many, the only way out of the cycle is to be caught and forced into accountability. The sad thing is that a way out could occur before that. The answer is found in yet another application of sorrow. The same misconduct can prompt either guilt or sorrow, and, as I have learned in working with many clients, one can be exchanged for the other. Guilt is self-centered. Sorrow, in response to misconduct, is other-centered. Guilt, as noted above, can hang on and move into a vicious cycle. Sorrow is likely to result in reconciliation or making amends. Why doesn't everyone ditch guilt for sorrow then? My guess is that sorrow is like a painful knife wound, while guilt is more like a dull ache that can be endured.

Let's take a moment and look further into bringing weightlessness into your ministry, a significant step in establishing a healthy ministry. *Weightlessness* is only a metaphor. It's a very useful one, but, like every metaphor, it breaks down at some point. Ministry will always have its inescapable heavy moments. When you have to bury a close friend or colleague, or when a tragedy occurs in one of your families, your heart will be heavy. But even in the midst of these moments is a lightness, a perceptible lifting of the burden that comes from the way people draw close to one another and the way in which God's comforting love seems to be especially present.

There are, to be sure, different kinds of heaviness. The one I want to focus on is particularly virulent and is never mitigated by people caring for one another. It is the heaviness of *resentment*— your resentment. Resentment is the opposite of weightlessness and will destroy the healthiness of your ministry. Your commitment to being healthy must include the understanding that you cannot allow resentment to stay with you in your ministry. The feeling of resentment is a sign that something is broken and needs to be fixed before moving ahead. The very first sign of resentment demands action.

So I ask the question: "What are you are doing in your ministry that you resent having to do?" Your first impulse may be to answer: "What a ridiculous question. I don't resent anything that I'm doing." I accept that as a natural first inclination, but I also know that when I ask people in ministry to consider the question from a deeper standpoint, there is always something—and on occasion a whole flood of somethings. High on the list may be the situation in which one individual is taking up an inordinate amount of your time, seemingly for no purpose. Let's call him Harry. Harry, a parishioner, is a nice guy all around, but he has the knack of finding you every day, whether in your office or elsewhere in the church, and engaging you in a conversation that seems to go nowhere. He appears to have an uncanny ability to work around any of your attempts to screen visitors, and his comments on the weather or the latest sitcom he has seen go on interminably. You have a million other things to do, and by the time Harry finally leaves, you are ready to scream.

Let's say that, at this point, you are ready to take health and excellence seriously. Something is definitely broken, and you need to do something. First, you need to begin with the operational belief that says "resentment can always be gotten rid of, it's your choice" or "where there's a will, there's a way." It is clear that you are not going to outmaneuver Harry. Hiding out does not seem particularly healthy! Start instead with the question: "Since I resent doing this particular task, is it really something I have to do? What would happen if I just didn't do it?"

At this point in workshops, an interesting discussion often arises. I start it off by saying, "No, you don't have to keep having these conversations with Harry—and you shouldn't!" Someone makes the obvious point that Harry is lonely, and isn't it my job to ease loneliness? Before I have a chance to say no, someone else pipes in with, "Isn't loneliness a form of troubled waters?" That is to say, isn't addressing loneliness the sort of challenge that we as ministers shouldn't shy away from? While I admit it is debatable, I would deny that loneliness is the sort of "troubled waters" that ministers are called to. Loneliness is in some sense a natural condition, and one that calls for friendship or companionship. You are in serious trouble as a minister if you set out to offer friendship to the lonely. Where would you ever draw the line? If it is your policy, as much as possible, to treat parishioners equally, you would spend almost all your time as a paid companion to the lonely. Unless that is your specialization in ministry, you would soon be filled with resentment. It may be appropriate to your role to help a parishioner deal with his or her loneliness, but for you to be the sole answer? No.

Using your creativity, I am sure you could fashion some way of cutting off your daily get-togethers with Harry. The one I favor most is the direct, transparent one in which you talk with Harry about your professional boundaries. Chapter 15 makes clear the importance of the boundary that says, as a minister, you cannot have friendships with parishioners. You could explain this in detail with Harry. You might even tell him that he is the kind of person you would welcome as a friend, but as his pastor, you cannot. You might also go on to help him face his loneliness and seek an appropriate solution that does not involve him checking in with you on a daily basis.

What if you decide that the thing you resent doing is not something you can drop? Then the challenge is to either change the task creatively—perhaps combine it with something you enjoy or find meaningful—or reframe your thinking about it. What if the resentment is not about a task but about a particular person (other than Harry)? Chapter 13 addresses that question more fully. But for now, let's just reiterate that resentment has no place in healthy ministry, and it is always possible to get rid of it. The best way of doing so is not to make it an internal battle ("I refuse to be resentful, and I will banish that feeling"). As is usually the case with troublesome feelings, we can just let the resentment go by acknowledging it, surrendering it, letting it dissipate, and then addressing the factors that brought it into being.

Exercise

The exercise for this chapter is found in Appendix A. Complete *Grade Yourself* (Appendix A) in the same way I ask workshop participants to complete it. Give a quick and intuitive response to each area. Then, to go deeper, pick one or two areas that caught your attention the most. These will be the areas of health that are most important to you at this moment. Make a specific plan to focus on improving your health—your wholeness, happiness, and weightlessness—in those areas.

PART 3

Excellence

CHAPTER 8

An Overview of Excellence in Ministry

As is generally true, we need to start with a clear definition of our terms—in this case, the term "excellence in ministry." How will you know if you have reached excellence if you don't know what it is? "Excellence" and "ministry" seem to go together intuitively. What could more demand our most superlative effort than the work of the Lord, the work of the church, the spreading of God's love to the world? Yet "excellence" carries some baggage; it connotes something perilously close to one of the seven deadly sins, *pride*. And, as many of us know, pride often comes along with *perfectionism*, but it is often burdensome for us and those around us. That is why we need to define our term carefully.

Wouldn't *faithfulness* be a better word? It doesn't have the problem of sounding like pride. The fact is that the definition of excellence will be very much like faithfulness. Then why not use *faithfulness?* I find that, because it's not often employed in ecclesial contexts, the term *excellence* is a wakeup call to clergy. Tell the average clergyperson, "You've got to be faithful," and you'll get a ho-hum response, or possibly a defensive response. Tell clergy they've got to be excellent, and you have their attention.

When you start to consider excellence, you typically begin thinking about how to measure it. For example, one might think that ministry can be divided into skill areas that include biblical knowledge, preaching ability, pastoral care, and administrative gifts for a start. Then we could develop a means of determining a proficiency grade for each of those skill areas. I suppose that twenty-five seminary professors listening to every one of your sermons over a period of two years (wouldn't that be fun?) could arrive at a meaningful grade for your preaching ability. Or just take the top scholars from each class, call them excellent, use a sliding scale, and end the discussion. Obviously, all of this is ridiculous thinking. We need a definition of excellence that has nothing to do with grades—one that is not about pride, or ego, or a certificate that proves you are better than anyone else in town.

Very simply, excellence is defined by the results of your actions—the *impact* made on others. You can preach the most eloquent and erudite sermon, but if no one is moved, then the sermon has not achieved excellence. One clear implication is that you do not own excellence; it always requires relation to others. You may have a very big part in it, but the impact that determines excellence is always outside of yourself. The intent is yours, the effort is yours, but you do not own the impact. Any attempt on your part to do so would have to include manipulation, or dominance, and denying others the freedom to respond as they choose.

Intent is closely related to impact. But it also signifies something that you can and do own, something that you can take full responsibility for. You *intend* to do exactly what is most likely to bring about an excellent impact. Your excellence is there, harbored in your intentions. The next chapter on the First Principle of Excellence is about two ongoing intentions. Holding faithfully to these two intentions encompasses everything that you could possibly do in regards to excellence in ministry. Just two intentions, you ask? That sounds too easy. It is easy in one respect, and difficult in another. It's easy in that anyone can adopt the intentions and carry them out. What makes them difficult is that at least one of the intentions involves a new way of thinking. When people finally do get this principle, what I have generally heard is: "Why didn't someone tell me this before?" or "Why didn't they teach us this in seminary?"

One other implication of defining excellence as impact is that we cannot always know or measure our impact. In other words, we are rarely aware of whether or not we have contributed to excellence or had a positive impact. Nevertheless, one of the best things we can do for the sake of the effectiveness and integrity of our ministry is to seek to understand as much as we can about the impact of what we have said or done. I often recommend to ministers beginning their tenure at a church that they preach a sermon in which they essentially tell people that they don't want to waste their time, and so they describe their intentions in preaching—that is, the impact they would like to have. It could sound something like this: "I want you to become more and more aware of God's love for you, and to feel more and more called or challenged to spread God's love wherever you can in your world." Then I suggest that they urge people to tell them whether or not that is happening, and to do so on a regular basis.

Granted, sometimes you will know your impact without being told. If you set out to convince Mr. Hatfield that it would be good for him to apologize to Mr. McCoy and bring an end to the feud that has deadlocked the church for thirty years, and he does it, then by all means rejoice. Call it excellent ministry. Treat yourself to a hot fudge sundae or take your loved one dancing. But don't take your success too seriously. Tomorrow, your brilliant words may fall on someone's deaf ears, and excellence will be gone.

This leads to one other implication. Excellence is not a plateau that you reach as a place to stay. It comes and goes; it is dynamic. But—and this is the important thing—your intentions can remain and be consistent. If you see to that, then the points of excellence to which you contribute will occur more frequently and will ultimately connect in a whole and holy ministry that has made a difference.

Exercise

Survey your past experiences in ministry and select one time when you felt that what you did was excellent. Write about what happened in the experience that contributed to the excellence. Consider every factor you can think of. Write about those contributing factors. Then think about how any of those factors might apply to and benefit your present ministry. (It will be interesting to note, as you read further, the extent to which those factors correspond with the Three Principles of Excellence.)

CHAPTER 9

The First Principle of Excellence
The Separation of Self and Role

Though it was decades ago, I recall as if it were yesterday the furor caused by one sentence uttered by a visiting preacher during a seminary chapel service. The furor lasted throughout the day and well beyond, with 100 percent agreement: everyone was incensed by what he said. Nevertheless, what he said is a close cousin to our First Principle of Excellence: "In ministry, sincerity is a second-rate virtue."

Beware the advice often given to fledgling pastors: "Just be yourself and you'll be fine." Through the role plays of situations in ministry that candidates participate in, I have learned that ministry often calls for something quite different from doing what comes naturally, different from being polite, different from just being ourselves. You might think of "just being yourself" as equivalent to "just being the guy or gal on the street." But if you are on the operating table ready to have a delicate procedure performed on your body, you would not want the surgeon to suddenly hand over her tools to the guy on the street. It is the same in the profession of ministry if we are to pursue excellence.

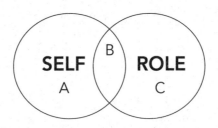

Self

The Venn diagram at left sets up this principle. Areas A and B together represent Self; areas B and C together represent Role. Area B is the Overlap between Self and Role. In simplest terms, the First Principle of Excellence in ministry means keeping the bad stuff of your Self out of your work. But that is hardly adequate to cover the thousands of rich applications of this principle. If I were to tell you to keep your Self out of what you are doing, you would look at me the way Casey Stengel's Mets looked at him when, on the first day of spring training, he reportedly told them to line up alphabetically by height. It would make no sense and, if you tried, you would end up catatonic. In terms of a doable and conscious procedure, the principle is asking you to remove any *self-concern* or *anxiety* that is unrelated to the task at hand. This means putting out of mind your worry about your car being overdue for an oil change, or what you are going to buy your spouse for your anniversary, or your son's failing grade in math. Also put aside your desire to make a good impression, your wanting to be liked or thought of as clever. "Clearing the decks" of these concerns is an important step in being able to offer the immediacy described in Chapter 1.

Separating Self from Role will take some effort on your part. During the early stages of practicing this separation, your inner coach will be highly active and verbal. Having to stop and go through the process of separating Self from Role will slow you down and, during this time of seeming inefficiency, you may wonder if it is worth it. Before long, however, it will seem natural to you and become a part of your Self—the area B part of yourself. And you will see that many things that are habitual and automatic can be very positive in your life.

Self-concern also runs deeper than your immediate worries. A good many of us have what are called "narcissistic wounds." For example, we have fixed in our minds that in childhood we did not receive the amount of attention, appreciation, or love that we deserved. Obviously, the reality supporting this belief varies greatly from individual to individual. Along with that loving attention we are convinced we did not receive, we believe it was necessary to our full development, and so the lack of it is responsible for many, if not most, of our deficiencies. Our unconscious "logic" then tells us that we need, with varying degrees of desperation, to make up for that loss. The attempt to do so enters surreptitiously into our actions with others and into our decisions about what we will do. Others, as they relate to you, will feel an obligation, perhaps unconsciously, to give you continual reassurance, praise, and affection. Over time, this can become heavy and draining for them, and it's not difficult to see that, if this happens in the context of your ministry, your ministry will suffer.

The same narcissistic wound, unless you become aware of it and control it, causes you to be reluctant to do anything that might arouse disapproval. Courage in your ministry thus has an enemy within and is severely inhibited. Knowing yourself well, and that these wounds exist, is vitally important. The importance of the emphasis that seminary education has placed on self-knowledge cannot be overestimated, and students would be well advised to take advantage of it. Bringing into awareness your narcissistic wounds does not necessarily make them go away. However, it does give you the opportunity to apply this First Principle of Excellence and remove them from your ministry to a great extent. Awareness of these wounds also gives you the chance to assess the reality behind them and to manage them in a responsible way.

There is one catchall of letting go that is effective in separating even the narcissistic wounds of Self from your Role. We concluded in an earlier chapter that letting go is important to health; it is no less important to excellence. We have referred to letting go of self-concern as the foundational step of the First Principle. Letting go obviously includes letting go of the worries that are in our conscious thinking. For self-concern that is ongoing and unconscious, one basic letting-go maneuver can effectively neutralize it. Here I resort to personal testimony.

Growing up I somehow managed to internalize a deeply imbedded message that said, "Whatever you do, it won't be good enough." I don't spend a lot of time thinking about it, but when I look back on my behavior, I see that this largely unconscious message has made a significant impact. Early in ministry when I was preaching regularly, I was generally useless during the time between when I had finished preparing the sermon and when I actually preached it. Believing, unconsciously, that it was not good enough, I obsessed about how to make it better right up until I stepped into the pulpit.

There were two solutions to this problem, but I never considered the second. The first, chosen by default, was to wait until the last minute—Saturday night—to prepare the sermon. Sleep that night would be fitful as I continued to obsess, but at least I wasn't totally useless Monday through Friday. I didn't stop to consider how the Sunday morning congregation would get short-changed by a haggard-looking pastor delivering a hastily prepared sermon. The second solution would have included the skill of letting go. How would I do that? Again, there are two approaches. One would be to get into psychotherapy and work back to the origins of my feelings of inadequacy. Then, with the help of the therapist, I would do what is necessary to let it go. It's a perfectly reasonable approach, and I would recommend it. A second simpler and quicker solution would be to employ a kind of self-instruction that can pretty much set aside all of the unconscious self-concern: "Let go of your self-importance."

The separation of Self and Role takes guilt out of your Role. Pastor Blue's failure (from Chapter 5) to distinguish his Self from his work is what makes it possible for guilt to take such a strong hold on him. Guilt is personal; it is about Self. You are in your work, but you are not your work. You may be guilty, but working harder does not get rid of or diminish guilt. If you are completely identified with your Role—that is, if you do not separate your Self from your Role—then your self-worth hangs totally on what is going on in your work or ministry. If guilt is what motivates you, you hang onto it for dear life. If it goes, so does your self-worth.

Role

Separating self-concern from your actions in ministry is half of the story. The other half is creating your Role. What do we mean by Role? Generally speaking, Role has many connotations and meanings, often including factors outside yourself, such as your job description and ironclad expectations of you. Our use of Role is more limited and specific; *Role refers only to what you decide and what you do.* You create your Role. To be sure, you do not create it in a vacuum; you include consideration of your job description and the expectations others have of you. But your Role is totally your responsibility. For the most part, the Role we are talking about is made up of a continual series of individual acts that, according to the First Principle, follow a certain rule. That rule is as follows: *Always chose to do the thing that is the best course of action you can arrive at in the present, for the sake of the effectiveness and integrity of your ministry.* No other aim, no other purpose should be allowed. That should be your intent. As long as it is humanly possible, and as long as it does not violate your boundaries (including those ultimately designed to protect your health), that is what you do. It should be clear by now that saying "but that just isn't me" is not an excuse when considering your Role.

When I was working at the Midwest Ministry Development Center, I spent a good bit of my time reading autobiographical questionnaires filled out by ministers and candidates. One of my favorites contained two sentences innocently placed back-to-back by one young male candidate for ministry. In the first sentence he stated: "I think perhaps one of my greatest difficulties is that I am indecisive." The second one went on to declare: "I say that, however, with a certain hesitance." It took me a while to recognize the brilliance of what he wrote. We *should* hesitate to conclude that any weakness we see in ourselves is the final word. I have often wondered if that candidate eventually came to realize the promise of his back-to-back statements, and if he came upon the First Principle, realized the reality of section C in the Venn diagram, and despite his indecisive Self began offering decisive and excellent ministry. I hope he did.

The question remains: How do I determine at each moment what will be the best thing I can do for the effectiveness and integrity of my ministry? The many unique factors of any situation you are in, combined with your ability to assess what is going on, surely enter into that determination. Although Chapters 15 and 16 will provide clear guidelines for making that determination, each pastor has the responsibility to reflect on the particularities of their context and choose how to apply those guidelines.

An Objection

In workshops someone almost always raises an objection to the First Principle. It is related to the uproar over the notion that sincerity is a second-rate virtue in ministry. It goes like this: "Isn't this principle telling us to do something contrived, not genuine, not spontaneous?" I'm surprised when this question does not come up; I've asked it myself. Here is the gist of what I give in response: What can be more *genuine* than trying to offer at every moment the best effort in ministry that I can come up with? As for *spontaneous*—the best explanation I have ever come across for this word is that it is the opposite of automatic. Being spontaneous is acting out of *choice*. Role, as we are using the term here, is that free, intentional choice that allows for the freshness and uniqueness of the present moment; in every moment you are making choices to intentionally act out of Role and not out of Self. Our Self amounts to what we know of ourselves already, and all our data comes from the past. "Just being myself" evokes the impression of something automatic, confined by the past—a passive acquiescence to my self-concerns.

This brings me to one of the most important strategies made possible by the First Principle. Even more important than unlocking courage you never knew you had is the opportunity for using *operational beliefs*. An operational belief, as we discussed in Chapter 4, is simply a belief you *choose* to hold primarily because of its impact on your behavior. Even if you are not entirely sure that you believe it, you act on it as if it were true. And you always do this because it is in line with the best thing you can think of doing for the effectiveness of your ministry. In other words, there are moments when love trumps even sincerity. I will give many examples of operational beliefs in Chapters 12, 13, 14, and 15.

Sister Angela

Everything I've written so far about the First Principle of Excellence could be just as well summed up by the story of someone whom I'll call Sister Angela. Sister Angela provided for me the one most unforgettable moment of my thirty-eight years with the center. A number of years ago, another staff person and I flew out to the east coast to conduct a three-day workshop for a group of Roman Catholic sisters. During our flight we were deliberating how to open the session. We decided that we would gather the forty sisters in one big circle and ask for someone to volunteer as a guinea pig and come to the center of the circle. I don't recall exactly what we were going to have the volunteer do, but we built up the invitation so that it would take considerable courage to volunteer.

We were making these plans on a crowded early-evening flight. Two things occurred on the flight that I later interpreted as God saying to me: "Wake up! You are about to enter into an experience I don't want you to miss!" The first unexpected experience was a spectacular sunset—at twelve-thousand feet in the air, I witnessed one of the most stunningly beautiful sights I have ever seen. The second experience that God used to prepare me to be open to the unexpected is a little more complicated. I was sitting in the aisle seat. My colleague was sitting in the middle seat, and a distinguished-looking gentleman sat to her right in the window seat. We were busy reading personality inventory results and confidential autobiographical materials that the sisters had completed. At one point my colleague became aware that the man to her right was peeking over her shoulder from time to time. So, she closed her folders and began a conversation with him. At first, following his inquiry, they talked about her work. Then, turning the tables, she asked what he did. I will never forget his reply: "I work for the CIA." Both of these experiences were preparing me to be open to the unexpected.

As for Sister Angela, I was reading her materials and was struck by her personality inventory scores, which showed her as being extremely introverted. Her autobiographical statements were written in a tiny scrawl that implied: "I don't want anybody to notice me or know who I am." I said out loud to my colleague (and I remember every word exactly as I said it): "I'm not a betting man. But if ever there was a sure thing, I have found it. I would bet every penny I own and every penny I will ever own that Sister Angela will *not* be our guinea pig." That evening we gathered the forty sisters in a circle and issued our invitation as planned. Only one hand shot up. It was Sister Angela. As I later reflected, I sensed God rebuking me for failing to be open to wondrous possibilities—and for being arrogant.

As it turned out, Sister Angela was in my colleague's group, so I did not have a lot of contact with her during the three days. I did have a chance, however, to ask her: "Why in the world did you volunteer that first evening?" Her reply: "I came into this experience wanting to find out what it would be like being someone other than myself. Your invitation to come to the center of the circle was my opportunity right off the bat." I did not need to ask her what it had been like for her. I could tell by the beaming smile on her face. I also knew then, for the first time, why my colleague and I had chosen that way of beginning the workshop. Sister Angela was obviously able to let go of the Self she had known and enter into a new and exciting Role.

Exercise

Draw a large Venn Diagram showing Areas A (Self), B (Overlap), and C (Role). What are the parts of your Self (Area A) that you need to be especially aware of keeping out of your ministry (Role)? List those in Area A. What are the parts of you that you especially need to include in your ministry (Overlap)? List those in Area B. What are behaviors (à la Sister Angela) that you would consider "not you" but could be important in your Role? List those in Area C. Recognizing that the contents of each area will change from time to time, focus on your immediate work situation (what you will be facing within the next week). Since each area is likely to contain an unlimited number of possibilities, focus on what might be most important with respect to your current situation. Note that what you list in Area C is an opportunity for growth—for increasing your competence.

CHAPTER 10

The Overlap
Self and Role Together

Shakespeare notwithstanding, you are not an actor on the stage. You are a person. You were a person before you checked in at Little Church Five Miles from Coon Hollow and you will be a person after you check out from First Magnificent Church of Metropolis. And hopefully you will remain a person in between. You are not an automaton.

Area B (the Overlap) of the Venn diagram is important and deserves its own chapter. It is a safeguard against the overzealous follower of the First Principle of Excellence who would try to ditch everything of his Self. If you were to take *everything* of yourself out of your Role, which would be impossible, you *would* be an automaton. Your attempts to represent God's love in the world would be unconvincing, confusing, or perhaps even damaging. Suppose you encounter a person whose life has been tragic and who has never known love. You tell that person about God's love, but she experiences your care as contrived and devoid of real feeling. Your Role, however skillfully played, comes through only as a stage role. She may leave still feeling empty and hopeless, no longer expecting to experience God's love for herself. Your Role of representing God's love needs your natural warmth, that genuine caring that is part of who you are.

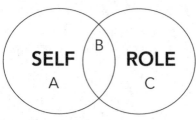

After you have removed self-concern and anything else which distracts you from being truly present, what is left? Just a lot of your unique quirkiness. And it is all your quirkiness—the little mannerisms that are only you—that make you, and your message, real to others! A thousand little things about you that you have little or no control over, that you are blithely unconscious of—they are what make it possible for people to identify with you, connect with you, feel close to you, feel affection from you and for you. Do keep these things in your Role—as if you had any choice!

So far we have been looking at parts of you that automatically end up in Area B without your being conscious of it. But a very important portion of Area B is formed by your conscious planning, and it involves some of the most important decisions you will be making. Our *boundaries* are a significant part of both our professional competence and our self-care. The limits that we put on ourselves define our character, offer safety to others, and secure our own health. Those boundaries must be a part of who you are, not just part of your Role. Remember, Role is something that is created over and over again, with the possibility of something new and fresh and better each time. Boundaries are in place, stable, and unchanging until the need for revision or addition comes along. Put simply, if you avoid lying, cheating, and stealing *only* when you are in your Role, your ministry will come tumbling down. And God help your friends and family! In the midst of being courageous and going into troubled waters, you must always bring along your boundary that assures you will not allow yourself to be either abused or killed. Short of martyrdom, which I have yet to recommend to anyone, it is always a part of your effectiveness and integrity in ministry to live and work another day, whole and intact.

The ongoing question in ministry is: What from your own experience do you share in your ministry? We are not particularly good judges of what is good and what is bad in our life experiences. Mistakes that you have made and painful experiences that have happened to you, which seemed terrible at the time, can turn out to be some of your best learning and character-building moments. Without them, you would not be the person you are. In a real sense, then, you could pronounce all your past experiences as being both irreplaceable and *good,* since they have all contributed to forming *you.*

Viewed in this way, all your experiences are of potential value to your ministry. The challenge is to determine what to share and when. Let's say you have made what you consider to be a terrible mistake at some point in your life. You may go for years without seeing any purpose for sharing that experience in your ministry. Then one day you find yourself listening to someone who is so anguished about something he has done that he feels he cannot bear continuing to live with himself. As it dawns on you that his mistake and yours are really the same, you decide that *now is the time* to share from your own experience. A life may literally depend on it.

Let's take a moment and look at the idea that all your past life can be used for good in your ministry. You not only can make that assertion, you *must* if you are pursuing excellence in ministry. Human nature seems to include a desire to push away from the occurrences that have seemed painful in our lives—to forget, deny, or disown them; to somehow go on without them; to dissociate them from who we are. When we do that, we diminish ourselves. When I am meeting with a distressed pastor who has a layperson in her church who clearly wants to get rid of her, I almost always recommend the following operational belief: *You are not the issue; that layperson, deep down, wants to get rid of a part of herself.* The intent is to shift the pastor's orientation from the weak and powerless states of anger and fear to the promising state of thinking in terms of pastoral care. (In Chapter 15 we will look at how pastoral care can proceed in such instances.)

Let's look further at what happens when you disown a part of your history. You gain some pseudo-relief by pretending that something did not happen. You then begin to apply the same coping technique to other painful experiences in your life, and you end up with a life history full of holes—like Swiss cheese. Not surprisingly, your sense of security and, in fact, your sense of yourself, begins to feel unsubstantial. You become fearful, nagged by the possibility that something will happen that will require more psychological "surgical" removal. That kind of fear quickly becomes intolerable, and you deploy the most common defense against fear—anger. Anger and projection typically become intertwined. Your way of dealing with yourself internally becomes focused outward, and you begin wanting to—and believing you can—get rid of things externally.

One of the most common manifestations of this in the church is when a pastor becomes set on a course of action that he or she believes needs to be initiated in the church. The pastor gets locked into one way of convincing the people to go along with the new vision. The people resist and the pastor blames the people for being unwilling to change. What is most likely happening is a projection of the pastor's unwillingness to change the approach and consider other ways of presenting the project or vision. When the pastor is able to be insightful enough to realize the projection, it becomes possible to keep the vision alive and accomplish it, while bringing people together rather than creating division. Blaming others kills the vision.

A great deal can be gained by embracing your whole life as good—the good and the bad. Sometimes this takes going back to a past event and working hard to accept what happened by looking at the good things that have resulted from it (e.g., the increased capacity for self-reflection and self-compassion resulting from working through a painful betrayal). If you look hard enough, the good things are there (note the operational belief). When you can embrace your whole life as good, at least two positive things occur. First, almost by definition, your self-esteem increases. If everything that has gone into creating you is good, you are as good as you possibly can be. Second, you become far less fearful. If you know that whatever experience you encounter will ultimately be good, what is there to fear? You become bolder and more confident. You become a *whole* person.

In deciding what from your own experience to share, there is one particularly important part of your life to consider. As a clergyperson, you will certainly be expected to speak from time to time about your own faith journey, and those moments can be times of great opportunity. They also are times calling for acute discernment. The stakes can be high. Everyone I know who takes faith seriously has at least one thing in common: their faith journey has been what you could call "all over the map." Rocky roads and dark tunnels of doubt have interspersed times of smooth sailing. My brightest and best clients, in spite of their excellence, have not been immune to difficult times. Many have shared with me their "dark night of the soul," and I have seen that at those times their separation of Self and Role has stood out as the only thing that kept their excellence going.

In deciding what to share of your own faith journey, you will want to avoid making it sound too easy, too good to be true. But you also will want to steer away from presenting something so dark and convoluted, so mired in your own issues, that no one else can understand let alone benefit from it. I would make a case, however, for leaning toward the latter. If excellence is our goal, the decision of what to share from your own faith journey is made from an acute awareness of where the people you are serving are in their faith journeys. If you don't know, then you are "shooting in the dark." But from what pastors have told me, those occasions to hear their people speak from their hearts about their own personal faith are much more limited than you might think. You might be surprised by how many of your people desire your approval (some, no doubt, believing it to be equivalent to God's approval). You might be even more surprised at how many would not want to risk that approval by sharing the dark realities of their journeys. Instead, they turn to the basics of a memorized creed or a replaying of what they have heard in your recent sermons—all detached from their real experience. You may be able to cut through this charade (as I hope would be your intention) through an honest sharing of your own struggle. In addition to learning more about what is true for your people, deepening their trust in you and their trust in the importance of truth may also be a part of your intent.

The bottom line is this: Everything you share of your own experience must serve the ultimate goal of contributing to the effectiveness and integrity of your ministry. What you choose to share in any given moment must be the *best* thing that you can imagine sharing to advance that goal. Taking the word *best* seriously will almost always push you to expect more of yourself.

The Overlap Area (B) that combines Self and Role is also the avenue for your growth. Highly courageous acts, initially existing in Area C (a part of your Role only—"I would never see myself doing that!") often move into Area A over time. They become part of who you are. In this way, your Role feeds your Self. Your Self is expanded, and your Role contains only the best behavior you could conceive. This becomes even more important in your retirement. When you finally leave First Magnificent Church of Metropolis, you will no longer have the same Role for yourself. That is when you will find that much of what has been your Role is now firmly lodged in your person, your Self. You will be more loving than you once were. You will have a greater desire to help others than you once had. You will also have more freedom to choose how and where you apply those qualities. And you will learn the secret of meaningful life in later years, which is to get outside yourself and find your favorite way of being generous in the world. That is what happens, at least if you seek *now* to embrace the Principles of Excellence.

Exercise

Consider your own faith journey and the current instances of challenge or opportunity in your ministry. Write about possible connections that would bring some part of your faith journey into the overlap of Self and Role. Write out a plan for effectively sharing that part of your faith journey in a way that will positively impact the challenging areas of your ministry.

CHAPTER 11

The Personal Benefits of
the First Principle

The First Principle of Excellence—the separation of Self and Role—works two ways. It benefits your ministry, and it benefits your personal life. Here's how:

1. *You do not have to take criticism of anything you do in ministry personally.* It is impossible to overestimate the importance of this fact. When things go wrong, you are not personally implicated. It was a decision that was wrong or a solution to a problem that didn't work. Decisions come and go. They can be changed. They can be managed with more attention to detail in the future. New ideas or solutions can be applied. They belong to the Role you have chosen. They are not a part of who you are. The only part of you that was involved was your *intention,* which, if you sought to do the best thing possible for the sake of the effectiveness and integrity of your ministry, is beyond criticism.

2. *You work with a greatly expanded tool kit.* This is obvious. Your intention to do the best thing possible for the sake of your ministry causes you to reach beyond your Self and employ courage, for example, that you never knew you had. You intentionally set aside thoughts about your limitations as you chase the best outcome for your ministry. In a sense, the sky is the limit. It seems clear how this will benefit your ministry, but you may wonder what makes this a *personal* benefit. The answer is in your satisfaction. Consider the difference between tackling a home project with one small hammer, a single screwdriver, and a miserable pair of pliers and taking on the same project with all the tools

available to a master carpenter. With the latter, you not only end up with a far better finished project; the work itself is a lot more fun, more satisfying, and far less frustrating. The personal benefit is that this expanded toolkit allows you to go beyond your own limited view of your abilities, which boosts your self-esteem, which gives you the courage to use the toolkit in other areas of your life.

3. *You spend a significant portion of your time free of the stress of personal concerns.* When you set aside self-concerns such as worry about people criticizing your sermon or finances, you enter into a space that is lighter, freer, and more beneficial both to your physical health and your emotional health. It is comparable to losing yourself in your work. To be in that space for a whole work day, day after day, prolongs life and refreshes you. I have been around sports long enough to know the health dangers of excessive fandom. However, I believe that something about being physically present in the stadium, watching your team play, is beneficial to health. For that period of time, you are so caught up in what is happening that you totally forget your own self-concern, and your stress level diminishes. Your day at work in ministry can be much like attending a game. Forgetting, or intentionally setting aside, self-concern lowers stress and gives you clarity of mind to function better in your role.

4. *You avoid making stupid mistakes.* Obviously the twenty-minute honeymoon of Chapter 3 would have been avoided, as well as others that cost jobs. One minister I counseled got "crosswise" with the bride's mother during the wedding arrangements. He did not like the mother of the bride and, during the actual wedding ceremony, in a part of his homily where logic would have had him say that "the couple was attracted to each other," what came out was "at least he did not find her butt-ugly." Had he heeded the First Principle of Excellence, he might not have lost his job the next day! When I hear of mistakes of this magni-

tude, I begin to think in terms of intentional (if unconscious) self-inflicted firing. But you can probably think of things on a much smaller scale that you have said that you wish you could take back. You can probably see that you said what you did when you were feeling greater personal stress than usual.

When you work with the First Principle, in a sense you are going through a process of *purifying* your product. You are choosing not to do anything unless its purpose meets the specification. One of the ways in which this purification process comes in handy is when you are thinking about sharing something personal about yourself in a sermon, for example. If you cannot identify a purpose for doing so that clearly contributes to the effectiveness of your ministry, it is probably wise not to do it. Otherwise, it may be received as an attempt on your part to gain either admiration or pity.

5. *You are saved from enduring useless, irrelevant, and damaging evaluations.* I have sometimes thought that pastoral evaluation procedures employed by many churches were brought to us by the same people who designed racks, thumb screws, and water tortures. I have seen copies of evaluation forms sent out to congregation members asking them, in effect, to rate the pastor on a scale ranging from "inadequate" to "downright disgusting." Of hardly more use are the ones requesting that you "describe what you like best about our beloved pastor." Better to begin by stating your intentions, and in your leadership role make sure that the evaluation of your work is based on those intentions. In this way you cut through the inconsequential opinions and preferences of your evaluators (criticizing the color of your socks, for example) in order to truly analyze your effectiveness in your Role.

When the evaluation team starts with the understanding that your constant intention is (a) to remove your self-concern from what you are doing in ministry, and (b) to carefully select the course of action that is the best you can offer, then the evaluation will not only be fair but also extremely helpful to you.

First, you can be evaluated in terms of how effectively you keep your self-concern out of your ministry. It obviously will not help you much to be told, "Well, I don't think you do that very well." But if someone starts out by saying, "I have noticed one thing you do that seems contrary to that intention," then it promises something that you need to know and that could be very useful to you. Note that just because you are the one being evaluated doesn't mean that you must abdicate your leadership. At that moment, the best thing you can do in ministering to your church is to insist that the evaluation be useful—useful to the church and useful to the ministry of the church. Whether or not it is pleasing to you personally is irrelevant.

Second, you can be evaluated on the correspondence between what you intended when you carefully determined your best course of action, and what, in the eyes of others, actually resulted. Understanding the gap between those two factors is invaluable to you and certainly can be approached through this kind of evaluation. Things almost never turn out exactly the way you expected—and sometimes they turn out even better!

Not all evaluations are official—although some "parking-lot evaluations" can carry considerable weight concerning your salary or tenure. Everyone is evaluating you one way or another. Even those wild and loose evaluations are more likely to be helpful to you if you share your intentions publicly. If they know that you consider surprise, for example, to be an important aspect of leadership, they are less apt to think of you as a loose cannon who has gone off his or her rocker when something unexpected occurs. Having shared your view on surprises, they are now likely to have some perspective that will help them respond to future surprises in the way you would hope.

6. *You can actually have a life of your own.* You don't have to be a full-time saint. Tending that boundary between work and leisure gives you the freedom to have a life of your own. Without

intentionally protecting this boundary, you might not have it. I have known more than a few clergy who have been burdened with the notion that they have to live up to the image of what a minister is in the minds of their parishioners even when those parishioners are nowhere in sight. Brian's practice (from Chapter 5) that enabled him to be high-up among the brightest and best— the practice of virtually forgetting he is a minister when he is off work—was his entry into a personal life of superb self-care, which in turn richly fed his ministry. This is Health and Excellence in a nutshell.

I recall one client who struggled with this. He was well-known in his denomination and highly respected. He also carried that fame and respect as a monstrous personal burden. When he came to see me, he was mired in a high-level but frustrating and unre-warding position. He told me of an opening that amounted to the ministry position he had always dreamt of having. Furthermore, he was qualified for the position and knew that if he applied, he would have a good chance of getting it. But the astonishing thing was, he was not planning on applying. Together we traced the rea-son to my old friend: guilt. There were other sources, but after a great deal of hesitance, he told me about his habit of swearing. He confessed to me that in private, especially while driving, he said he lets loose with the most vehement and vile profanity ever to leave anyone's lips. He tortured himself with the thought "if they only knew!" I totally shocked him when I replied to him with, "I'm glad you do that" (meaning the swearing, not torturing himself). I went on to say, "You are under so much pressure in your job that I'm glad you have at least some form of release. It probably keeps you sane." In this instance, my intent worked. He went ahead and applied for the position.

7. *You grow in ways that make you a much better person.* As we have been noting throughout, when you stretch and do things for the sake of your ministry that you previously thought were not

you or were beyond your capabilities, they eventually become part of you. To the extent that you abide by the First Principle of Excellence, those new things are always positive. In choosing to love in your ministry, you become a more loving person. In choosing to act with courage, you become a more courageous person. Again, this becomes all the more important when you consider retirement. There will come a time when you will no longer have a professional Role in ministry. But that does not mean you will stop loving or acting with courage because they are not required. Loving and acting with courage will become part of you, and you will find yourself wanting to find outlets for that love and courage. Only, at this point, you have more freedom to choose those outlets.

Exercise

Choose the one area of personal benefit discussed in this chapter that strikes you most or that appeals to you most. Journal about it, stating why it appeals to you. Describe how you can employ the First Principle of Excellence in a way that will maximize this benefit.

CHAPTER 12

The Second Principle of Excellence
Always Choose Strength

The Second Principle of Excellence is to *always choose to take the strongest position or action that you can.* We saw in Chapter 4 that when excellent ministers choose how they will conduct themselves in ministry, they do so from a place that can be referred to as their "depths." There they find three things: individual differences do not matter, anger disappears, and a sense of peace prevails. As we explore in this chapter what it means to choose strength, we will find that it is closely related to these three things.

I have learned from workshops that I need at this point to say what strength is *not,* or else I will lose some people. Strength, in our context of excellent ministry, is not brute force, manipulation, intimidation, using the authority of our office to gain advantage over others, or throwing a punch at Mr. Grumble in the middle of an administrative board meeting (it's been done!). Strength is neither defensiveness nor aggressiveness.

The following twelve Rules of Strength give a clear picture of what *is* meant by strength in our context. The first one is the most important.

Twelve Rules of Strength

1. *Strength is knowing and reminding yourself that, whatever the outcome of any situation, you will be okay.* The source of this strength brings peace and is ultimately spiritual. For access to that

76

source, I would urge you to read Romans 8 over and over again, each time trying to allow yourself deeper access to the knowledge and feeling that Paul had. This particular strength allows you to let go of any preferred outcome from whatever you are doing. You may want to give it your best effort because of how much you care (which should follow from everything said so far), but things do not *have to* go your way. You leave others with total freedom to make their own responses. That is respectful, and that is strong. If you are in a conflict, you do not have to win. *Weakness* is the inflexible need to have things go your way. A person who has to win—who cannot stand to lose—is a dangerous, desperate person and is in a severely weakened position. Conflict almost always brings with it the possibility of a really good, perhaps unexpected, outcome. (Be wise enough to count on it and it will happen!) But when one of the parties cannot bear to lose, it never turns out well.

Finally, you will likely always be in a strong position if you do the following: Carefully plan what it is you would do if you suddenly no longer had this job. Go about it not with a sense of desperation but with a sense of anticipation, even fun (but don't have so much fun that you quit your job). Make it something really good. Talk it over with your family. You never know when the moment might come when your own self-respect (lose that and you lose everything) compels you to take a stand that the lay leaders in your congregation cannot accept.

2. *Strength is acting out of kindness and love.* Where kindness abounds in any relationship, that relationship can withstand an enormous amount of stress. It can tolerate disagreements and live through conflict. *Weakness* is acting out of hate or meanness. Where hate and meanness prevail in a relationship, the relationship is brittle, and cooperative effort is all but impossible. The Third Principle of Excellence is all about this strength, so I will leave the elaboration of it to the next chapter.

3. *Strength is always attributing the highest motives to other people regardless of their actions.* This one is an application of rule number two. It is also a prime example of utilizing an operational belief. The others on the list seem to be common sense. For many people, though, this one probably is not. Yet I believe this one is extremely important. But, you say, wouldn't this make you naïve, vulnerable to surprise attack? No, it wouldn't. To understand this better, it is helpful to distinguish between motive and action. Think back to the last time you were misunderstood, and you will see that they do not have to be the same. We see people's behaviors; we can only guess at their motives.

Attributing negative motivations to others immediately creates a dynamic of "them versus me." I am the reasonable, well-intended person; they are selfish, untrustworthy, or even dangerous. I would never drive like that! I would never post that kind of comment online! But the truth is we are all a jumble of mixed behaviors and motives, so seeing the best possible motive in someone else's behavior is a way of reminding ourselves that the circle of human virtue and frailty includes all of us. Rather than "them versus me," there is "us."

When we encounter people who seem to be hateful, the point is not what our assumption about their motives does to them—at least not in the short run—but what looking at their motives in a different way does to us. If we do not follow this rule of strength, we descend into the world of hate ourselves. *Hate poisons our spirits and diminishes every other strength on this list.* We are left in a weakened position. And our chance of becoming peacemakers evaporates. *Weakness,* therefore, is considering only our immediate, surface, and often fearful reaction to what others are doing.

When we attribute the highest motives to people, it increases a hundredfold our ability to live and work with them. It makes us effective in our ministry with them. The discussion of gossip in Chapter 14 will examine this comparison in more detail.

4. *Strength is helping others take the strongest stand they can take for themselves.*

I used to become uneasy whenever I was asked to work with two pastors on the same church staff who were at odds with each other. The request usually came not from the pastors themselves but from a third party or entity such as a personnel committee. The expectation was that I either help them resolve their differences or authoritatively report that the situation is hopeless. My first problem was that I never wanted to resort to the latter. My second problem was that, while both pastors would publicly agree that resolution was a good thing, deep down either one or both were unwilling to reach an agreement. That, of course, sabotaged any hope of resolution. Given their public stance, many might conclude that the problem was, of course, my failure to deliver.

That all changed when I finally figured out what to do. When I finally chose to apply the Principles of Health and Excellence to conflict situations, I actually started looking forward to those opportunities. What I did was spend some time privately with each individual, introducing them to these Rules of Strength and helping them work out how they wanted to apply them in the current situation. Then I pretty much sat back, occasionally encouraging and reminding them to stick with the Rules, and watched as they together worked out their own resolution—one that was creative and mutually satisfying.

I came to believe that if we encourage all parties in a conflict to articulate their positions from a place of strength, as we've outlined above, then a resolution is likely to emerge that is beneficial to all. Even if you yourself are on one side of a conflict, excellence is possible if you help the other side take as strong a stance as possible. Needless to say, it can be a very meaningful part of your ministry to help people use these Rules of Strength for themselves. And imagine what would happen to the church if all your lay leadership were introduced to the rules and followed them.

Weakness is hoarding health and excellence for yourself, believing its benefits are intended only for you, the pastor.

5. *Strength is being open, direct, and transparent.* This, of course, does not mean laying your entire life out for all to see. Within the realm of your ministry, whatever you share of yourself should have a purpose related to ministry. This Rule of Strength relates directly to your intentions. Being open with your intentions is certainly to your advantage, but it also helps others. They know who you are and why you are doing what you are doing. Their trust of you grows rapidly with your openness. Accordingly, people will grant you a great deal of leeway as long as they know you are being guided by your stated intentions. In seeing clearly where you are headed, they will know better how they might join you or support you. And far from least in importance, if people know your intentions ahead of time and have some qualms about them, with your encouragement they can let you know before you get started. This is a much better option than letting you know in the middle of a crisis or, even worse, after it's too late.

It is also helpful for you to be crystal clear about your boundaries—to take initiative in communicating those boundaries and the reasons for them. That way if, for example, you do not accept out-of-the-way personal favors, the ones offering them will know why instead of taking your rejection as a personal affront.

Weakness is being indirect, beating around the bush (as if you want others to take responsibility for guessing what you would rather not say), or operating with a hidden agenda. What is hidden generally comes out in the open and, feeling tricked, people have second thoughts about trusting you. It's far better that you are direct and open so that people don't have to wonder, "What does she or he really mean?"

6. *Strength is knowing and honoring your own limitations.* Here we need to be selective in what we mean. Certainly knowing the limits of what you can do or endure physically is impor-

tant (listening to your body). But we have already cautioned against being too quick to think we are limited in such matters as courage or decisiveness. What is most important here is honoring limits to our *privilege* and our *importance*. People, especially those who are in the church, are inclined to think of the clergy as special and to grant them privileges, allowances, and importance. Strength is tied to your boundaries—the boundaries that tell you not to take advantage of any of these. *Weakness* is buying into the notion that because you are the minister, you have special importance over and above other members of the community of faith.

I have often been asked, "When should I let them know I will be leaving?" This is an individual matter, and I generally try to help the inquirer look carefully at his or her individual circumstances. The question itself ultimately prompted what I think is the best answer: right after you arrive at the church! Here is the scenario: Shortly after you begin your ministry at the church you call a meeting of all the lay leadership. You say to them something on the order of the following: "I want to talk with you about my leaving. I know I just got here, and I hasten to add that I'm not thinking of leaving anytime soon. But when a pastor does leave a church, it can become, in many ways, a make-or-break time for a congregation. We can begin to do things together, starting right away, that will ensure a healthy transition, whenever that time arrives, as well as ensure our strong working relationship between now and then. Our focus together should be on what is good for the congregation.

"So let's look at the reasons why I might leave. First, I might die. That would not be particularly helpful to the congregation. I want you to know that my intention is to prevent that from happening. And there may be times when I will want your assistance in keeping that from happening. I hope you would be willing to offer it.

"Second, there may come a time when some—maybe many—believe I am not the right person for this church. At the first sign of that, as it comes to your attention, I would urge you to let me know. I can change, if we agree that I should. If the matter becomes serious, I would ask that we discuss it thoroughly *and come to agreement*—an agreement that we can present to the rest of the church. If, however, you and I cannot come to agreement, this is what I promise will happen: *Since you are clearly more important to this church than I am—you are the church, I am not—I will honor your stand and present to the congregation the fact that I honor and trust your wisdom.*

"A third possibility would be that I feel called somewhere else. Pastors have been known to blame God when what they really mean is 'I want out of here.' At that point I would want you to question me hard. If it's a matter of me wanting to run away from something difficult, that's not okay, and if you think that's what is happening, I want you to let me know.

"Finally, my ministry here could run its course. I might have given everything I have to give you. You probably will know that before I do, and I would not want you to hesitate to say so. Over our years together, we may develop warm feelings for each other. You may actually grow to like me! Stranger things *have* happened! When the time comes for me to move on, I would want you to stand firmly behind what you believe to be best for the church. If your feelings for me are no longer the warmest, there is no question about what you should do, what I would want you to do, and what I would expect you to do. We're in this together!"

7. *Strength is taking responsibility.* If knowing that you will be okay, no matter what, is the most important strength, this one is a close second. It is also the hardest, and the one that potentially can have the greatest impact. To use this strength fully requires working with a different concept of responsibility than we are accustomed to. If we claim to belong to God's family, then we are responsible to and for every creature under God's heaven. We can choose either to own that responsibility or not, but strength

means owning it. We have been taught to accept some pretty far-fetched things (like if a butterfly flaps its wings in Melbourne, Australia, the temperature in Nome, Alaska, is affected). If you can believe that, then you should be able to believe that if a child dies of starvation in Mali, I am responsible. And it should be an easy step from there to say that I am responsible for everything that happens in the church I serve.

"But that is ridiculous," you say. "I didn't even know the child in Mali." That is true. But there is an infinitesimal bit of logic that says that I lived on the same planet at the same time as the child, and I *could* have gone there and saved her. But logic is not the point at all. It is a frame of mind. As a child of God, I am connected to all of God's other children. I can choose to believe that every one of God's children who is in need has a claim on me. It's not that I will always meet that need; what I am able to do is finite. But the point is that, regarding any one of those needs, I *could* respond. If I don't, I am still responsible.

That may be interesting as a philosophical point, but what does it come down to in practical terms? Where is the strength? Obviously, recognizing my responsibility for the child in Mali does not do her any good, nor does it help her family. What it comes down to in practical terms is a matter of *witness*. As others observe me taking that responsibility, it tells them that I care about such occurrences, and that, feeling responsible, I will *want* to act. I will feel a kind of deliberately chosen obligation to act when I see a need within my reach. The witness to responsibility, more than anything else, is an implied promise. There is far too much of an attitude of "I am not responsible" in our midst. I am not responsible for the poverty in the inner city. I am not responsible for so many people being homeless. I am not responsible for the terror the gangs are causing. That claim of no responsibility is the root of the fragmentation in our world, in our communities, and even in our churches. In response to the witnessing of responsibility, the hope would be that, like my reaction to my friend Dick at the football stadium (Chapter 6), people would feel: "That is the way to be; that is the way *I* want to be."

Weakness is blame. When I botch the job of nailing something together, I am inclined to blame the hammer and get angry with it. If that insane way of thinking crosses over into the rest of my life, I become the personification of weakness and incapability. For example, Joe, a layperson in your church, is given a critically important task and, like me with the hammer, he botches it. Weakness on your part would be to say, "Don't blame me. It's not my fault. Joe should never have done it the way he did." Strength would be to say, "I bear some responsibility here. I could have given Joe some support, but I didn't. I could have worked alongside him, but I didn't. He had every right to expect me to, but I didn't."

The kind of responsibility we are talking about here is a mature responsibility—a responsibility that stems from acknowledging our connection with others, that is, an extension of our care that's not based on guilt or obligation. Taking on this kind of encompassing responsibility would imply saying thousands and thousands of times, "I could have, but I didn't." If each of those times were accompanied by guilt, the burden would be unbearable; we would be paralyzed. Sadness or sorrow is understandable, but guilt becomes the enemy of responsibility.

8. *Strength is being patient.* You can divide the activities of your life into two categories: the trivial and the important. You can address trivial responsibilities in a hurry. But when something important comes along, strength is about saying, "Take all the time you need." I don't mean to denigrate the trivial. Add up all your trivial responsibilities (even brushing your teeth) and you probably couldn't or wouldn't do without them. But for the most part, dealing quickly and efficiently with them saves you precious time to spend on the truly important things. When Joe comes into

your office looking worried and starts beating around the bush, strength is *not* interrupting and saying, "Get to the point, Joe. I'm very busy." As his concern starts to unfold, it often takes time for the real issue to become apparent. One of the biggest wastes of time is when we take off running after a red herring. *Weakness* is dawdling over the trivial and hurrying through the important.

Time is something that we easily fall into hoarding. Take my time away from me and you take my life. Schedules and clocks are important, probably necessities in our world today, but make sure to hold them both loosely so that they do not control you and interfere with the quality of your life or ministry. The truly important often comes up as a surprise and needs both time and patience to come to fruition.

9. *Strength is being active, doing something.* This one can be in creative tension with the previous principle. Wisdom is in deciding which strength to employ in any given situation. Some things need to be left alone, that is true. Deciding to do nothing is, in fact, doing something if it is an intentional action. The important thing is to make that decision and then move on without looking back. Issues come up—disruptive, inconvenient, annoying issues. Do not linger in unproductive annoyance. Plan to do something, sit with your plan long enough to be confident in it, then do it! *Weakness* is endlessly brooding, worrying, and sinking deeper and deeper into passivity. Procrastination, guilt, worry, fear, and self-concern all get in the way of being active, of acting from a position of strength.

10. *Strength is inviting critique.* Try conducting ministry from a closed cell with the lights out. That is exactly what you are attempting when you try to hide from criticism. Strength, as we've said before, is being open with your intentions, asking people to help you by appraising your intentions, and then asking them to let you know when your actions do not seem to match your intentions. You will appear strong when you give this invitation and

85

then receive those who take you up on it with genuine grace and appreciation. What is most impressive, though, is when it becomes crystal clear that you have taken the critique seriously, either by acting on it or by discussing it at length with your bene-factor. *Weakness* is seeking only praise or positive feedback and attempting to remove yourself from any situation where you might be criticized.

11. *Strength is inviting others to join you.* There is strength in numbers. To say to yourself, "I'm the only one who can do it" is not only arrogant, it is weak. Some parts of ministry are mundane and, let's face it, boring! Inviting others in on those parts is called delegating. What you call boring may be someone else's cup of tea. That's okay, but it's not what I mean here. Other parts of your ministry are challenging, intriguing, fulfilling, even exciting. Inviting others to join you is a gift to them and a gift to yourself. If something is challenging, intriguing, fulfilling, and exciting, it adds immensely to your pleasure to share it. *Weakness* is flying solo, believing you're the only one who can do it right.

12. *Strength is listening deeply.* The church, perhaps more than anything else, needs to become a *listening* church to fulfill its mis-sion. The pastor needs to set this course. Everyone's experience is unique. Everyone's point of view is unique. We generally try to sim-plify things by putting what we hear into static categories so that we don't have to listen so hard or so deeply. A button gets pushed and a little message tells us, "I've heard all this before." We tune out, which causes us to miss a lot. This sequence imperils many marriages. *Weakness* is ultimately listening only to ourselves.

Everyone's inner distress imprisons them in loneliness until someone finally truly listens. Not expecting that anyone will want to hear, people shut off their real inner voice, the voice that would say what is truly important. Pretense, fakery, diversion, and gossip become the means of avoiding silence and too often the common mode of talk around the church. "Build it and they will come"—that memorable line from the movie *Field of Dreams*—is our reminder. Choose to listen deeply—shutting out everything else (all other appointments, all preconceived notions, all thoughts of your own)—and they *will* talk. And the product of that talk can lead to improved relationships and the ability to love and be loved.

But the most important application of listening deeply has not been mentioned yet. We practice the idea that prayer is about asking God for what we want, or in our public prayers asking God for what will sound like what God would want us to want. I believe that the most important part of prayer is listening, listening to what God is saying. It takes enormous quiet to do that. It surely takes going into our depths.

This list of strengths is a starting point. Many more can be added as you practice living out the Principles of Health and Excellence.

Exercise

Choose one of the Rules of Strength that particularly strikes you or appeals to you. Write it down and state why you have chosen that particular strength. Then, during the course of the day, look for an opportunity to apply it. Later, journal your impressions, evaluating how well you utilized the strength, and what impact it had. Challenge yourself to apply a new Rule of Strength each day for the rest of the week.

CHAPTER 13

The Third Principle of Excellence
Straight from Jesus—"Judge Not"

A few years ago a member of our board of directors, an Episcopal priest, gave me some invaluable advice. He said that in every church there is one truly wise soul who will not be easy to pick out. When you first arrive at the church, take the time to find that person. The truly wise soul is often (but not always) a woman. She has much to offer you. God has given her to that congregation so that, even in the most dysfunctional situations, you'll have a beam of light, a thread of hope—God's remnant, if you will. How do you find her? She generally is well along in years. She is quiet and patient. She is almost never in a position of power or authority in the church. She sees things differently. When you do find her, go to her with your thorniest problems, your deepest dilemmas, your dark nights of the soul. She can be what some call a "spiritual friend," a person with whom you can have a deeper level of conversation, perspective, and reflection. You will not be disappointed. If, however, you have looked and looked and have not found her, look for the one who does not judge.

Jesus told us to not judge others (Matthew 7:1-2; Luke 6:37). This is the Third Principle of Excellence. This is the key, the "simple" step, in being able to love all your people. To understand this, we have to rely on theology or perhaps an operational belief. Our operational belief is this: created in God's image, we have a natural ability to love—one that is in some fashion or another similar to God's love. Only we tend to deny it, twist it, or block it in some way so that it is not always evident. It is through our judgments, our condemnations, that we block the love God intended in us. If we are able to remove those judgments (would Jesus have told us to do so if it were not possible?), love would be effortless and natural. Put this to the test. Imagine someone in your church whom you find difficult to love. Try removing all your judgments about that person and see what is left. Keep going. Take a whole day and catch yourself each time you start to make a judgment condemning someone. Stop yourself, withdraw the judgment, and see how you feel.

When we judge someone, we give up our power to work with that person or to minister to that person effectively. Conversely, if people come to us in their guilt, fully expecting to be judged (already condemning themselves), and it is obvious that we are not judging them, their surprise turns to gratitude and a sense that they have received God's grace. And they have.

In my first Health and Excellence workshop, we had a long discussion about this. One pastor spoke about having to remove a young man from being the head of the youth program of the church because of some ethical misconduct. He said that he had to judge the young man in order to do his job responsibly and see to the welfare of the youth in the church. After much deliberation, we arrived together at the point of agreeing that you have to make difficult decisions or judgments in carrying out responsibilities, but you do not have to condemn. The best part of what happened in this discussion, I thought, was that the group helped him go back and reconstruct what he might have done. As it had happened, it had turned out badly. The young man felt angry—belittled and betrayed. Several of his friends left the church with him, feeling injustice had been done. In the reconstruction, the group started with asking the pastor to identify and then withdraw any judgments he had made about the young man. From there, the pastor found it easy to describe what he would be able to do. As he described how he would handle the situation given a second chance, what stood out was the care and understanding he was now extending to the head of the youth program. He did not back down from his decision, but fully explained his reasons in a way that avoided judging or condemning him. He was able to suspend personal judgment so that he could make the decision required as a leader in a way that reflected the love of God.

When we withdraw our judgments of others, what is left is trying to understand them. That in itself is loving. When we reach the end of our understanding and still don't quite get it, the best thing to do for the sake of ministry is to move to an operational belief: the person I don't quite understand is doing the best he or she can, given his or her life circumstances. This, of course, is applying the third Rule of Strength. Typically, because they care deeply, people in ministry have strong personal views on issues such as abortion and homosexuality. I think it is fair to say that we spend time judging and condemning those whose views are opposite ours. It would not be too much of a stretch to set those judgments aside and begin to look for ways of understanding where those persons are coming from. That does not mean that we will change our views, or theirs, but unless we set aside our judgments and attempt to understand, we will never learn to live peaceably in a church, or in society, where people are allowed to think for themselves.

A few years ago I attended a conference and heard the speaker, a psychologist, say something that I thought was astounding. He claimed, "All diagnosis is projection." Although perhaps not intuitive at first, what he was telling us was no different from the common saying, "When you point a finger at someone else, you are pointing four more back at yourself." The more I thought about it, the more sense it made. We cannot fully understand something in another person that we haven't first experienced in ourselves.

Many times I have used this claim when advising pastors to reframe their thinking about the person in their church who wants to get rid of them. I encourage them to think about that person as someone who really wants to get rid of a part of himself or herself. To adopt this operational belief, and do it in earnest, is to automatically shift from a position of anger and defensiveness to a position of wanting to extend pastoral care. If you act out of a desire to provide pastoral care, what you will generate in the other will follow an early progression from surprise to confusion, and then perhaps just maybe on to self-understanding and healing. Once begun, this Third Principle can send things off in an entirely different direction.

One implication of "all diagnosis is projection" is that when we judge others, we are doing something to ourselves. Our harshness toward others may actually be an attempt to avoid harshness toward ourselves, but it doesn't work. Conversely, when you begin to withdraw your judgments of others, you will become less condemning of yourself. Self-condemnation fuels guilt. Whether it is projected outwardly or felt inwardly, it is a significant problem in ministry. I am thinking now of two individuals who were as gifted as any ministers I know, but who suffered breakdowns because of brutal, intense self-judgment. I knew the reasons for one. It was intolerable for him not to live up to and surpass the accomplishments of his father. The other individual I felt I got to know well, yet I never had a clue why he was so hard on himself. There seemed to be no reason (but no doubt there was). Loving yourself and loving others go hand in hand, as the gospel suggests. That is why letting go of your judgments and loving your people is the best thing you can do for your health—and it doesn't hurt your ministry either.

Finally, what I consider to be the ultimate in operational beliefs for ministry is a spiritual discipline that invites us to consider every act directed toward us as either one of two things, and nothing else. *Either the act is an expression of love or a call for love.* Imagine the quality of your ministry if you stayed with that belief at all times.

Exercise

Take a full day to be acutely conscious of your judgments and condemnations of others. Each time you are tempted, work on withdrawing the judgment. As soon as you can, journal your reflections on what happened when you withdrew judgment, how it impacted you, and, if possible, how it impacted the other person. At the end of the day, write your reflections on how the day went for you. Was it different from other days? Keep going with withdrawing judgment tomorrow and beyond.

PART 4

Do You Really Want to Do This?

CHAPTER 14

Three Applications
Gossip, Weddings, and Routine Pastoral Calls

Health and excellence do not take place in a vacuum or at a comfortable retreat center. They come into being in real settings in ministry, amidst ordinary and sometimes aggravating events. I have included three such ordinary and aggravating events here and three more in the next chapter. I hope they benefit pastors who are dealing with these situations so they can follow the path of health and excellence in ministry.

Gossip

Gossip happens in the church, and it can be very destructive. Like dynamite, it can destroy in a moment what has taken months or years to build up. I'm not surprised that I often hear the question: "How do we deal with gossip?"

Gossip is a form of criticism. From experience, you undoubtedly have learned that there are two basic types of criticism: criticism designed to help you succeed, and criticism designed to help you fail. More than once I have sat down with a desperate clergyperson who has shown me a long list of things the church wants him to correct, criticisms that are buzzing around in the back channels of the church. I recognize this as a form of gossip right away and try gently to help him become aware that this list is impossible. There is no way he could ever do it, and it would be fruitless for him to try. It would play into the purpose behind the list, which is to make him so anxious, or tie him in such knots, that he would give up and leave. Some other strategy is called for.

Gossip is a favorite weapon among those who want to get rid of you. Gossip, of the kind where you are the intended victim, is certainly of the second type—the type designed to help you fail. Needless to say, whenever you receive criticism of either kind, it is in your best interest to determine which kind it is. The key to approaching excellence while dealing with gossip is to treat both kinds in the same way. Apply the third Rule of Strength: "Always attribute to others the highest motives." Hopefully, the following makes clear how that works.

Suppose you become aware that gossip is spreading that you are having an affair with the church organist. This is not true. What you can do is call a meeting for as many of the congregants as can attend. You address them as follows: "It has come to my attention that there is a rumor going around that I am having an affair with our organist. I want you to know that I was quite dismayed when I first heard this." (This much is to let them know you are only human.) "But after thinking about it, I was glad to hear it." (You now have their full attention—remember the importance of surprise in leadership.) "I was very gratified to know the people of this church care deeply about the *integrity* of our ministry in our church, and I invite them to come forward and work with me to see that it is not compromised in any way. By the way, the rumor is not true. But I know that perhaps this rumor came about because something I did led to this impression. Whatever that was, I would like to know what it was because I recognize that it was a threat to the integrity of ministry here. I'm glad there are others who are concerned with the integrity of the church as well, and I invite you to speak with me if you see me doing anything that compromises the ministry here."

We can enumerate the Rules of Strength, in addition to Rule 3, employed here. You would be doing something active, taking charge instead of slinking around worrying about who is spreading the rumor and who is believing it. You are taking responsibility. ("I must have done something.") You are concerned about the integrity of the church's ministry, not about blaming someone of misperceiving or manufacturing false information. You have invited participation through offering to work together on your common care for the integrity of ministry in the church. Throughout, you held to the First and Third Principles of Excellence. Not once did you communicate real concern about yourself (your Self) or imply judgment on the gossip of the church. From the moment you talked about feeling glad to hear the rumor, your communication was all about the integrity of ministry.

Also, you may well have gotten through to those who wish for your failure that they cannot defeat you easily—at least through gossip. It may make a difference in that their view of you may now shift to one of grudging respect. Perhaps they may even go beyond that and respond to your invitation. A new and very different type of relationship may begin. From what I have often heard, those times may be the strongest you will have in ministry. What is generally reflected is the two-step process of excellence: for a brief time chaos reigns, and then the pieces are rearranged into something new and positive. It is important to remember that none of this positive change would be possible without you courageously making the move to deal with the gossip directly.

The Wedding

I have frequently asked the question, "What do you like least about your ministry?" I'm surprised by how often the response is "weddings." Maybe I shouldn't be surprised. Horror stories from weddings abound. They don't teach you in seminary what to do when the bridegroom passes out in the middle of the ceremony, or when a bridesmaid catches her spiked heel in a floor register coming down the aisle and keeps going with the register following her all the way down to the front. Sometimes the music gets out of hand. "I'd Rather Have Jesus" may be good theology but is inappropriate for a wedding (even though the bride has requested it!). It is hard in such moments because you feel responsible for the dignity of the service.

Weddings can be difficult for everyone. Weddings often spotlight the brokenness in families, and that brokenness can give you an occasion for acknowledging and engaging that brokenness. Uncle Ned, who was like a father to the groom, is not invited because he is no longer married to Aunt Edna. The bride's father and stepfather have never been in the same room together, and everyone is on edge waiting—but not wanting—to see what happens when they finally are. Alcohol is thought to be the solution to dilute the anxiety, and it flows like at no other time or occasion. And we're back to the groom and half of the wedding party passing out at the altar rail (it has happened).

Here is what you do in your role as pastor. At some point prior to the wedding, you ask to meet with as many members of both families as can attend. Assembled, you tell them, "I want to make you an offer which you are free to accept or decline." You go ahead and tell them what has been your general experience of family brokenness and its role in weddings. And you go ahead and say, "I consider it part of my calling to try to bring healing when needed. I would be very willing to do whatever I can, and take whatever time it takes, to address whatever brokenness might be in your families. If you are interested, I can explain in detail how I think that might be done. This is something you should know: the brokenness in families is actually a stumbling block for the couple getting married. Making a good marriage is not easy; but it is often made that much harder by the brokenness in family backgrounds that has not been addressed. One of the best gifts you may give this young couple is to take me up on my offer." At that point what usually happens is the father of the bride steps forward and says, "Thank you, Pastor, for your kind offer, but there is no need for that as far as our families are concerned." And they all file out after him. Thirty minutes later you get a knock on your office door. As you open it, Aunt Edna stands there asking, "Pastor, can I speak with you?"

We have had some interesting discussions in workshops about what you might do if they do take you up on your offer. I won't go into detail here, but those discussions have generally come around to include considerable use of the Rules of Strength and the encouragement of family members to employ them. One final note: even if they do not take you up on your offer, they have heard, maybe for the first time, that the unhealed brokenness in their family histories may hurt the young couple. If that leads to something, of the many directions that they may go in, all directions would seem good and, therefore, evidence of a position of strength.

The Routine Pastoral Call

This application makes major use of an operational belief that can be applied to any pastoral contact or conversation. Routine pastoral calls are often high on the list of least favorite activities among clergy. Sitting in someone's living room not knowing whether you are really welcomed—while you have a thousand and one other pressing things waiting to be done—may be about the last way you want to be spending your time. As long as you have that attitude, it doesn't do much for the other person either.

This important operational belief makes all the difference in the world: there is a purpose behind all encounters. God has a purpose—an important one—for every encounter. Like sea turtle eggs, maybe only one in a thousand hatches and grows to maturity. But that's okay. God is patient. That one is worth the wait. If you believe this and are on the lookout for God's purpose, those odds naturally get better—maybe one in two hundred.

And so, because it is that important, you clear your mind of all else and prepare to try to discern what God's specific purpose is for your pastoral call. It's not easy. It's not meant to be easy. At the very least, it is an intriguing intellectual challenge—something high on your list of what you need to make your work stimulating, and even fun. It causes you to listen deeply to the one you are visiting—to listen for the meaning beneath the words, to use your empathy and your imagination, to feel some excitement in the quest. (Already this is a gift of no small importance to the other person.) In the interest of transparency about your intentions, you may say out loud, "It is my belief that God has a purpose for our being together today." You may also want to include the bit about the sea turtle eggs, and add, "It's usually not easy to know what that is, and maybe we won't find out. But maybe, too, we can work together to try to figure it out." If that is not an invitation to go deeper and talk about what is really going on, I don't know what is!

Imagine for a moment the impact on the other person. I would certainly expect that he or she would feel greatly respected and deeply cared for. And just imagine if, against the odds of two hundred to one, together you discover and fulfill God's purpose. The wonder and joy might almost be too much to bear, but you would settle for that!

Exercise

Prior to a pastoral call or other pastoral contact, determine that you will take on the operational belief that God has a purpose for this occasion. Before and during the contact, do all you can to open your awareness specifically to understand what that purpose is. You may want to share with the other person what you are doing and enlist his or her help by explaining your belief in God's purpose and asking that person to look for it as well. Later, write about the experience. What happened? How did it feel? What was the impact on the other person?

CHAPTER 15

Three More Applications
Conflict, Staff Communication, and Friendship

These next three applications are not necessarily about aggravating aspects of ministry. Nevertheless, they call for us to use the Principles of Excellence laid out in this book. Conflict, staff communication, and friendship, while not as overtly challenging as things we've covered previously, nonetheless require your attention in your journey toward health and excellence in ministry.

Conflict

I have already stated that conflict can almost always be resolved into something positive if everyone involved can be encouraged to follow the Rules of Strength. Let's see how that works. The Hatfields and McCoys have held the church hostage for decades, through five beleaguered pastorates. Yours threatens to be the sixth. Whenever any initiative or proposal arises for adoption, the Hatfields take one side and the McCoys take the other. The loyal sheep-like followers, about equally divided between the clans, follow suit. Nothing moves. Nothing gets done.

This is obviously a conflict that requires some excellence on your part. So, as a first step, you form your intention. What is the best thing you could do for the sake of the effectiveness of ministry in this church? After pondering this question, you decide that if you could get Ms. Hatfield and Mr. McCoy to work *together* on a project, that would give you the best chance of breaking the ice that has frozen this church for decades. So you either find or create a project that is important to the church—one that needs a high level of competence to carry out the research, design, and attention to detail required.

You approach Mr. McCoy first, describing the project and asking him to work with Ms. Hatfield on it. Included in what you say to him is the following: "This is the most important challenge and opportunity the church has faced in years, and it needs the best minds and leadership we can provide. That's why I want the two of you to work on it. Over the years, you have demonstrated a deep and continuous love for this church. You have unquestionably shown strong leadership. On top of that, I know you to be highly intelligent and resourceful people. I am confident that, together, you will come up with the best possible approach in getting this done. Because I have such confidence in what the two of you will eventually come up with, I will leave it to the two of you and not get involved in any of your planning."

Mr. McCoy, after hearing your request, responds, "There is no way I'm going to work with her." You are ready for this and reply, "In all the time I've known you, you've never been one to back away from a challenge. I said earlier that I won't get involved in your planning, except by offering support if and when the two of you run into difficulty initially—and I do believe it will only be initially. You need to know that I also have a great deal of confidence in the kind of support I will offer, and I know that we will get beyond any hurdles to get to the business of meeting this promising opportunity."

Note something at this point. The kind of support you are ready to offer comes, as we shall see momentarily, from applying the Principles of Excellence. A matter of no small consequence is your conveying—even more by attitude than by words—the confidence you have in the Principles. That confidence is analogous to the confidence a surgeon has in his or her training, tools, skill, and preparation. It becomes a force of its own and is contagious. It generates in others high expectations and the kind of confidence that brings out their best.

You go on to say, with both seriousness and a bit of amusement, to Mr. McCoy, "I, of course, talked this over with Ed (the lay leader of the church), and he agreed with me that the two of you would be our best bet. I know this would be a tough task to take on, but frankly, I think you are the kind of person who can manage it. Ed is confident in you and your strength as well and he's known you for years. I think he'd be surprised if you backed away from this because it was too hard for you." Mr. McCoy's response is not all that you hoped for, but it is enough for now and is sufficient to let you know he will be on board. He says, "Well, I'll consider it. Let's see first how Ms. Hatfield responds. I can't imagine she will want to work with me." And you say, "Oh, I have every confidence she will after I present it to her."

Later, after a similar approach to Ms. Hatfield, the Hatfield-McCoy duo begins their work together. Predictably, after their first session by themselves, an angry Ms. Hatfield approaches you. "I cannot work with that old goat. He keeps getting off the track by going back to old history and putting me down. It's just not working!" Again, you have anticipated this and say, "It's okay. I was prepared for this and know how to get us—actually, the two of you—beyond this point and into the heart of what I know you will be able to do so well. Hold off any conclusions until I talk with Mr. McCoy. If what I say to him doesn't work, I will let you know, and we'll go from there. But I can't imagine that it will not work!" (Note how your confidence stays front and center.)

You then approach Mr. McCoy and repeat what Ms. Hatfield has reported to you. Under the heading of "judge not," you say to him, "I knew from the beginning that you and Ms. Hatfield would first have to get past your contentious history to clear the decks for the important work you have taken on. I am pleased and grateful to you that you went right to work getting that inevitability out of the way. As I see it, you are now ready to move ahead. To help with doing so, there are some things I want to share individually with each of you."

You then go into teacher mode and describe the separation of Self and Role and the Rules of Strength—expanding on them only as much as necessary to see that he understands them and knows that you expect him to follow them throughout the rest of the course of this important project. Finally, you ask for his commitment. In the unlikely event that he would demure, you are ready with, "If you cannot make that commitment, I am prepared to ask Mr. Aaron to step in and take your place." You know Mr. Aaron to be Mr. McCoy's right-hand man in the church, and one who is eager to take on more leadership responsibility. He is also quite capable. He, too, commands the respect of the McCoy faction, and his participation would serve the same purpose you initially had in mind. You also know Mr. McCoy well enough that he would not tolerate that shift in limelight.

You take your same teacher mode to Ms. Hatfield so that they are both committed to the same set of expectations—expectations under the umbrella of Excellence. The rest is up to them, with perhaps your occasional reminder to them about the Principles. You have continually held to high expectations, both of yourself and of them. And the result very likely will be the healing of a long-term crippling disease in the church *and* the delivery of an exciting new project.

The Hatfield-McCoy episode above is one kind of conflict faced by pastors. Generally, a more challenging type of conflict is one in which you, as pastor, are one of the parties involved. Gulliver Grumble wants you out. Someone has warned you that Gulliver has been going around attempting to convince others in the church that it is time for you to leave. His latest dagger is the complaint that his wife, Gladys, was in the hospital for two days a month ago, and during that time her mother passed away in Pennsylvania. Not only did you not show up to visit Gladys, nary a word has been heard from you regarding her mother's passing. (Of course, you knew nothing about this. No one said a word to you about either Gladys's hospitalization or her mother's death. In fact, it came out later that when a friend heard what was going on, she said, "Oh, I must tell the pastor." Gulliver promptly told her, "Oh please, don't. The pastor is very busy and doesn't need to be bothered with this.")

When you first learned what Gulliver Grumble had been doing, for a moment you naturally felt dismay, fear, and anger. But you quickly formed an *intention* to handle the situation using the Principles of Excellence. Initially, your work will be with yourself. You might start by shifting to a certain perspective. I mentioned earlier that we are not particularly good at judging our own experience in terms of knowing what is good and what is bad. Instead of becoming anxious that things will end badly for you, Gulliver may be initiating something that could end up being a very good experience for you—and there's a reason for it. Your situation is somewhat analogous to that of an athlete. Athletes do not reach their best potential until they come up against the stiffest opposition. They are then forced to find the giftedness within themselves that they previously did not need. Gulliver may just be presenting you the opportunity to make some major leaps forward on your journey to Excellence.

Still working with yourself, you turn to the first Rule of Strength: no matter what happens, you will be okay. This includes reminding yourself that you will be okay even if you lose this job. You combine that with the third Rule of Strength: always attribute the highest motives to others. You have now helped yourself to set aside both your fear and your anger, and you have prepared, at some point, to say the following to Mr. Grumble: "Gulliver, I've watched you since I arrived here, and I know that you care greatly about this church. You want it to be the best it can be. I know you've been critical of me, and even that you think the best thing for this church would be for me to leave. I'm sure that this comes from your love for the church. The thing is, you may be right. I can't see it, but I also know that I can't see everything. If you are right, I would willingly leave, knowing that would be the best thing.

"I would welcome hearing your reasons, and maybe I will be convinced. Or maybe I need to make some changes that haven't occurred to me—changes that would make a difference in your thinking. If you don't want to share your reasons with me, or if you do but are not satisfied with the results, the next step would be to meet with the church council. You have every right to do that. The proper procedure according to our by-laws, as you no doubt know, would be for them to carefully consider what you are saying and then decide whether the matter is serious enough to bring to the body of the church for a vote."

You may have more to do at some point. At the start of this mess, Gulliver had pretty much shown that he will not allow you to pastor him—at least not without a major, life-threatening crisis. However, by virtue of the respect you have shown him in conveying the above, he may open that door a little. You turn to an operational belief that tells you basically that you are not the issue for Gulliver—that deep down it is not you he wants to get rid of, but something in himself. You take stock of what you know about him. His children have all left the nest and you've seen hints of alienation between Gulliver and them. His marriage seems okay, except you sometimes wonder if Gladys ever dares to have a thought that is different from his. You also know that something occurred a few years ago in his work that has been troubling to him. Somehow, something went wrong in the company he still works for, and he was blamed. People said he made a serious mistake. He wasn't fired, but his status has suffered ever since. You have the impression that from that time on, he has been passed over when the most important projects are handed out.

As we discussed earlier, you may have such intense negative feelings about something that has happened in your past that you want to disown or forget the experience. Your self-esteem suffers, and you become overly fearful—fearful of something similar happening that will be out of your control. The defense against that irrational fear is often irrational anger that gets acted out in various ways. Taking this into account, you may have the opportunity to inquire about that experience in Gulliver's past. You might encourage him to talk about what he did, but more importantly, the reasons he had for doing it at the time. You are still in the mode of attributing the highest motives, and perhaps you can help him see that he did only what he thought was best at the time— all that can be expected of anyone. This might well be the start of a healing process that will restore wholeness in Gulliver's life. What began as an intense conflict may well end in a significant life transformation. This may be the highest quality pastoral care you can provide to the members of your congregation.

In the end, note what happens in Gulliver's life as a result of your helping him understand and observe the Rule of Strength: Always take responsibility. Note also that, having completed this journey with Gulliver, you will have discovered new levels of strength in yourself that will serve you well in both life and ministry.

Staff Relationships

One of the favorite parts of my work has been team building with church staffs. I have worked with some great ones and have learned much from them. A very simple but profound truth I have learned is that staffs function better when the people like each other. Apart from natural chemistry, there are some things that staffs can do to facilitate that happening. Self and Role have something to do with it. It is pretty commonplace to hear top executives and heads of staffs of churches say, "I need to keep some distance from those working under me. If I let them get too close, they'll lose respect for me, and my judgment in making wise decisions may be compromised by my feelings for them. In short, we need to respect each other, but we don't have to be, nor should we be, best of friends." I agree with all of that, but only insofar as it is speaking from the standpoint of Role. Role has a great deal to do with good staff relationships, and I will get to that in a moment. But in the best staffs that I know, Self has also been very much involved. Role alone doesn't cut it. The best staffs get together on the personal side of the boundary between work and off-work. They have fun together, they play together, they enjoy food together. And they are equals in every way in the context of off-work, fun time. The head of staff is important in the sense that he or she turns the key and opens the door, and basically says, "Okay, we can go for it!" After that the head of staff is just like everybody else.

Had I not known these kinds of staffs, I don't think I would have placed top importance on liking each other. But I have known them, and I would not hesitate to say that I have sensed a strong bond of love among the best staffs I have encountered. Competition, except of the playful kind (the card game Hearts can get brutal!), is totally absent. Everyone is committed to helping everyone else do and be the best. Staffs like that, I can testify from experience, do face the normal run of crises and turmoil. But they do so with amazing tolerance for both stress and differences of opinion. And I'm convinced that the spirit in staffs like that spreads naturally throughout the whole church.

My work in Health and Excellence has led me to develop an offshoot workshop on staff communication in which I focus on separate modes of communication among staff. Being clear about which mode you are in, or you intend to be in, is key to avoiding much confusion, misunderstanding, and hard feelings. Awareness of the modes comes in handy. There are four, and they all begin with C. They are largely defined in terms of the question: Who has the power, and how much? The first is *Coordinator*. This mode usually belongs only to the head of staff. When the head of staff is speaking as Coordinator, he or she has 100 percent of the power. That is because the head of staff is the one ultimately responsible for the life of the whole congregation. Whatever is going on in the ministry area of any staff member must ultimately bow to the welfare of the whole church, and that welfare is the concern and responsibility of the head of staff. In the Coordinator role, the head of staff has the power to say no to staff persons, to pull them off one job and put them on another, or to create something new for them to do.

It's interesting to see how well the various staff can work with the Coordinator role. Is the head of staff able to step into that Role? Is the head of staff strong enough to say to an associate, "I know you don't like it, and I don't have time to explain to you why, but I need you to take care of something right away." Are the associates strong and mature enough to accept that kind of authority? Is the trust level of the team high enough that the whole staff can live comfortably—and appreciatively—with the Coordinator role? A final note: The Coordinator role is to be used sparingly.

The second is the *Consultant* role. This is my favorite, and one that, when used extensively, tends to characterize an excellent staff. Anyone on the staff can be a consultant to anyone else. Encouraging the Consultant role among church staff means that people on the staff pay more attention to each other's work, learn more about the whole church, and care for one another by actively helping one another. Furthermore, the work in each area of the church is likely to improve. The Rule of the Consultant role is that the Consultant has zero power (how well I know that!); the person whose ministry area is involved, the recipient of the consultation, has 100 percent of the power. This Rule is very important, or confusion reigns. Consider when the head of staff (let's say it is a man) comes to talk with the youth minister. Right off the bat it is absolutely essential to know whether the head of staff is approaching as a Coordinator or a Consultant. Otherwise, if he says to the youth minister, "It would be a good idea for you to take the senior highs bowling Saturday night," what is the youth pastor to do? If it is clearly established that the head of staff is coming as a Consultant, then the youth pastor should be free to say, "Not a good idea. We have a Bible study already planned," or something to that effect. And the youth pastor will proceed with her plan if she is healthy and mature. Those qualities lacking, she might say, (1) "Okay, we'll go bowling then" (weak), or (2) "Okay," and then stick with the Bible study (passive-aggressive). It is also a test of the head of staff's strength and maturity whether or not he is comfortable with zero power in the situation ("Whatever you decide to do is okay with me").

When a head of staff invites associates to be in the role of Consultant with her, the results can be beneficial to all. For instance, she calls one of them into her office and says, "This is the situation I'm facing. What would you do in my shoes?" Remember that you, the recipient of the consultation in this instance, have all the power. This can become an invaluable, no-risk learning and training event for both the associate and the head of staff. It's quite possible that the associate will have some ideas that have not occurred to the head of staff—much better ideas, in fact. If this happens on a regular basis, it can bring enormous benefit to relationships among the staff as well as to the entire church.

The other two Roles occur less frequently. One is that of *Collaborator.* When two staff members are working on a project that combines their respective areas, the power is split fifty-fifty. The head of staff may sometimes be involved with another staff person in a Collaborator role, with neither person having final authority. This can be an energizing or even playful counterpoint to their normal relationship pattern. Often this works best planning a special event that is outside the typical range—a unique worship service, an inter-generational or cross-cultural experience, etc.

The other is the *Challenger* Role. It should be understood from the beginning that if any staff member thinks another staff member is going off the deep end with something—including the head of staff—that staff member not only has the right, but also the obligation, to challenge the supposed deep-ender. There can be no power rule for this. In most cases, this is an occasion for the whole staff to come together to decide whether and how to challenge their colleague—especially if the deep-ender is the head of staff. In more serious instances, some other entity (such as the personnel committee or staff/parish relations committee) should be brought in. The other situation in which the Challenger Role may come into play is when a staff member believes that the head of staff, acting as the Coordinator, is asking for something to be done that goes against the staff member's conscience. Hopefully, the issue can be resolved between the two of them if the head of staff is mature and competent. I can't imagine a truly competent head of staff demanding that an associate act against his or her conscience.

Friendship

When I led boundaries workshops for pastors in the early 1990s, I often felt like Daniel in the lion's den. The participants' turmoil always rose to a crescendo when I told them they could no longer be friends with their parishioners. I could tell by their reactions that what they heard was: "You have to be distant and aloof with all your people." (Those who weren't outright angry seemed to be

practicing it on me.) I responded with: "No, that's not it at all."
After explaining as best I could the reason for the boundary and
the wisdom of adopting it for themselves, I suggested that they
could relate to parishioners in a way that still has many of the best
features of friendship, such as closeness, warmth, and generosity.
But it would not be true friendship in that friendship is a two-way
street. I can tell you my deepest secrets, and you can tell me yours.
I will be there for you, and you will be there for me. Friendships
that don't have that balance tend to drift away. The reciprocal
characteristic is the very essence of friendship. What you as the
pastor cannot do, according to the boundary you need to maintain, is expect or actively seek something in return for the care you
give to parishioners. You don't tell your parishioners your deepest
secrets, even though it can be appropriate for them to tell you
theirs. Your Role is to represent God's love in their lives. That not
only allows but also encourages you to be as close and caring as
you can be. But telling them your deepest secrets would cross your
professional boundary.

People will feed you, literally and emotionally. They may, out of
their own need or desire, shower you with praise and affection.
No one is asking you to shut the door on that. The fine line is
crossed when you expect it, need it from them, or actively seek it.
Crossing that line may not be something you detect easily. You
may have one parishioner who always makes you feel good about
yourself. That person unfailingly lifts your spirits. Over time
someone tracking your movements would conclude that you paid
more attention to that person, found more reasons to put that person on committees, and (if the tracker is perceptive enough)
sought that person out more frequently when you were feeling
down. Let me warn you: there always is a tracker in your church.
And that is how rumors get started.

Another way to look at this is that, whether you like it or not,
by the nature of your Role you do represent God to people. That

gives you special entry into their lives. But—and I imagine every minister has felt this at one time or another—it can feel like a terrible burden. Who can begin to be like God? And it separates you, makes you feel isolated and lonely. The temptation is to want to come down from the pedestal and say, "Hey, here I am, just like you," and then try to show it by dramatizing, even exaggerating, your humanness. What you are doing then is ministering to your own need and taking away that authority your parishioners need from you.

Anthony

The story of Anthony is tragic. He did not die, but his ministry did. You might have thought that Anthony was primed to be among my top clergy. He was immensely talented and had risen quickly to become head of a large congregation. He had tons of personality; people were attracted to him immediately. On top of that, he was very sensitive to others, quick to spot the first sign that someone might be troubled by something, and able to understand almost instantaneously. He was generous, even overly so. He would make an ideal friend. The problem for Anthony was that he made friends in the wrong places. He never did anything that would be considered immoral, but he caused a great deal of hurt and anger among some of his parishioners, and in the end he broke his own heart. He left suddenly, just walked away from it all.

Anthony worked very hard. His ministry was his whole life, except for his marriage. But apart from that he had no one else in his life. He needed friends. He recognized that. He was a people person. When he chose those who might be his friends, they were flattered, and they found themselves drawn into a close and rewarding relationship. They were also people in his church, and eventually he saw to it that they were elevated into the lay leadership. He was warned by colleagues that this was wrong, but he ignored them. To him, having these friends in the decision-making roles had served him well so far, and he wasn't about to give it up. He was convinced that this was the way he was wired.

Eventually the church faced a crisis and had to make a very important decision—and quickly. To say that Anthony was invested in the outcome would be the understatement of the year. The church decided Anthony needed to take a leave of absence in order to focus on self-care. He did not think he needed the leave. To him, a vote in favor of a leave of absence would be a slap in the face, and he knew everyone knew it. He was confident, though, because those who were in positions to vote were his friends. He overestimated their loyalty.

The First Principle of Excellence helped these friends separate Self from the Role they took very seriously, that of deciding what was in the best interest of their church's ministry. Almost to a person, they voted against Anthony and for the well-being of the church. He was stunned. He felt as betrayed as anyone I have ever known. "How could they do that?" He was clearly oblivious to the honorable integrity of those individuals and unaware of the agony each one of them had to have gone through to make the separation they made.

Anthony could not take it. He left the church suddenly without telling anyone. It wasn't the outcome of the vote that got to him; it was the sense of betrayal that he felt. Gone was the ministry he had worked so hard to build up, and gone were his only friends.

You Need Friends

You need friends. Doing excellent ministry does not exempt you at all from frustrations and disappointments. You don't have to win all skirmishes, but because you care so deeply, you experience deep feelings that would not be appropriate to share with anyone in the church. In most churches you'll find close to an equal number of extroverts and introverts. Even among the extroverts, the majority have substantial introverted needs. After spending all day with people, most pastors are ready to go home and pick up some solitary activity or hobby. The last thing on their minds is to go right back out and scan the town for potential friends. Many have told me, "I get my fill of relating to people all day long. I'm glad to spend time with my family later in the day, but that's all." I'm worried when they go on to say, "I get all my friendship needs met through my work." Either they are violating boundaries or they do not understand their friendship needs. Some will say, "My family provides me with all of that." I doubt that is true. That is too much to expect of families. The problem with families as far as friendship needs are concerned is the family agenda. For example, your kids have homework. After you spend time helping them with that, maybe only the dregs of the evening are left. You and your spouse have plenty of household chores, from meal prep and clean-up to paying bills and changing light bulbs. And then what can you do with the kids that's more fun than homework? Doing all that takes up a big chunk of time and energy. And it isn't fair to burden your family with the agonizing struggle you are having with someone they may sit next to in church the following Sunday. With friends outside the church, however, it is much easier to make friendship the only agenda.

The ones I feel for the most are the small town pastors. I say to them, "You need friends from town outside the church." And they reply, "There is no town outside the church. Take away my parishioners and no one is left in Gruesome Gulch." That is why I believe that one of the best things the church has done in the last forty years has been to establish peer groups for ministers, and I urge all the pastors from Gruesome Gulches to find one or start one.

Everyone needs full-fledged friendships of the reciprocal, two-way variety. Especially those doing ministry need them; and *most* especially of all, those doing *excellent* ministry need them. Or to put it more precisely, it is almost impossible for pastors to do excellent ministry without solid friendship networks that support their personal well-being.

Exercise

Note a current instance of conflict in your ministry (either one in which you are a party or one in which you are a bystander). Consider becoming involved in such a way that transforms the conflict into something positive. Carefully form your overall intention and, beginning with a description of the conflict, write it out. Then journal a plan to carry out your intention. Note how you will utilize the Principles in your plan. Note also which Rules of Strength are most likely to come into play. In journaling, anticipate one episode of significant resistance and describe your contingency plan for dealing with it. Extra credit: Now implement your plan!

CHAPTER 16

Two Applications to Current Ministry Concerns
Social Media and Financial Management

The challenges of ministry are changing at an accelerated pace as cultural pressures and technological innovations are felt in the church. Issues that were on the distant horizon fifteen years ago are now front and center. One might wonder, how do the Three Principles apply to these twenty-first-century concerns? We are currently hearing from pastors and denominational officials about two particular issues: social media and financial management. The use of social media has radically impacted our traditional understanding of personal and professional relationships and our understanding of healthy community. Financial management has recently emerged as a major concern for pastors, churches, denominations, and seminaries, as more and more pastors are finding themselves trapped in seemingly unsolvable financial quandaries. The Three Principles have a great deal to offer us in navigating these "troubled waters."

Self and Role Applied: Handling Social Media

Much can be (and has been) said about the place of social media in the church. Most denominations have developed guidelines for pastors in managing the ethics of their personal and the church's social media presence. Of course, the Internet is full of suggestions, warnings, and even commandments for pastors in this area.

These guidelines are generally aimed at preventing pastoral misconduct, either intentional or accidental. While this is a worthy
goal, a broader look at pastoral ministry and social media,
through the lens of understanding Self and Role in ministry, can
help us see how social media is both a positive opportunity and a
significant danger to pastors and those they serve.

We can begin with our basic understanding that the pastor's
personhood and the pastoral role are two deeply connected but
distinct spheres. The pastor needs to be aware of both spheres in
order to be healthy and effective in ministry. From this understanding flow two key elements for excellence in ministry
(Chapter 1), which are two sides of the same coin. First, always
do the best possible thing you can imagine doing in the present
moment for the sake of the effectiveness and integrity of your
ministry. In other words, expect a great deal of yourself in your
pastoral functioning, and do not let yourself settle for less.
Second, identify the self-concern that interferes with doing the
best possible thing, and make a conscious decision to let it go.
This basic understanding and these two principles lend themselves to some guidelines that can help pastors use social media
wisely and effectively.

First, pastors need two separate social-media presences.
There is no way to balance the complexity of Self and Role
within one Facebook page or one Twitter feed. One account is
for the pastor in the pastoral role; another account is for the
pastor as a person. The former allows the pastor to set aside
personal needs and focus on ministry impact. The latter allows
the pastor to be himself or herself outside of the pastoral role.
A cautionary note: nothing posted online can be assumed to
remain private. The pastor needs to remember that what is
posted in the personal account can easily leak into the public
sphere, so any personal material which is radically out of sync
with the pastoral role should not be posted. (And if one feels a

need to be the "anti-pastor" in one's personal postings, perhaps that urge should be shared in some other forum.)

Second, pastors have a responsibility to use social media well in their ministry. Some pastors love engaging with people on social media, while other pastors dread it. The former can become a social media addict; the latter can be a Luddite opposed to any use of social media at all. These personal preferences should have no place in how one actually uses social media. Pastors are to use social media in the best way they can imagine. Every decision to post, tweet, and accept a "friend" or a "follower" is to be guided by the Principles of Excellence. This means that one's decisions are made thoughtfully and with clear intentions, just as any other pastoral decision. The pastor needs to remember that people beyond their intended audience will end up seeing what they post online. Given our human capacity for self-deception, pastors will benefit from having people with whom they can process complex or unclear social media situations and people who can hold them accountable for what they post. Articulating to another person your reason for wanting to take a particular course of action can be profoundly clarifying. This Principle of Excellence in handling social media will also often mean that the pastor delegates aspects of social media management to others in the church who are more skilled in this work or have more time for it.

Third, the pastor needs to bracket and let go of issues of self-concern when using social media. Social media tends to "disinhibit" people, including pastors, and it naturally draws out urges and impulses that we typically keep under wraps. Do you long to have your fifteen minutes of fame on the Internet? Do you want to have a "big platform"? Let it go. Do you want to be viewed as insightful? As funny? As culturally "with it"? Let it go. Do you want to accumulate Internet friends and followers? Let it go. Do you want to impress people in your church? People outside of the church? Your ministry peers? Your mother or father? God? Let it go. It's important to know yourself and the ways you are tempted to distort and endanger your ministry online.

Fourth, pastors should take charge of defining their pastoral intentions regarding social media. It is up to the pastor to make sure that people understand what their pastor will and will not do via social media. For example, explain your stance and rationale for how you will deal with friend requests from congregants. Explain why you do not do pastoral counseling via instant messaging. Explain why, when you eventually leave your congregation, you will not use social media to pastor them from afar. Explain how you and the church will do everything possible to keep the youth of the church safe when they interact with either the church's or the pastor's professional social media site.

I offer one final note on social media based on our previous definition in Chapter 8 of pastoral excellence. Social media is having a tremendous effect on how people relate to one another and understand the nature of community, and that effect can be expected to intensify. People can connect with each other in cyberspace in amazing ways; however, people can also be absorbed into looking at their smart phones and ignoring others in the same room. You may be thrilled, appalled, or alternately thrilled and appalled by the changes in the social landscape. The church should be deeply invested in creating healthy community, both within its own membership and in the world around us, including the online world. Every social media policy and practice of the pastor and the church should be consistent with the goal of bringing the quality of "safe sanctuary" to the online world. An online presence that invites genuine community, where differences are acknowledged and explored with openness rather than hostility, would be a breath of fresh air. Pastors should not underestimate their capacity to help generate this kind of social environment for people. The Principles of Excellence demand no less.

Self, Role, and Choosing Strength: Managing Finances

Financial management is difficult for many people. Lack of financial literacy, pressures from a consumerist society to seek happiness through spending, unsolicited offers for credit, and a "live for today" mentality combine to push people into poor financial choices with long-term consequences. These consequences can be severe and cause a cascade of suffering that sweeps through the lives of individuals, families, churches and other institutions, and even whole communities. When we consider how this affects the church, we might hope that robust spiritual lives and deeply held values would protect people of faith. However, pastors regularly witness the damage that poor financial management wreaks in their congregants' lives. This is a serious problem that deserves a serious pastoral response. So why is it that pastors usually evade this topic, or offer the superficial promises of the "prosperity gospel"?

It may be that pastors have so little to say because their own financial lives are in such disarray. We frequently meet with pastors on the brink (or over the brink) of financial crisis. Large debts (due to student loans and consumer spending), vagueness or outright denial about their financial situation, unconscious and unhealthy assumptions about money, lack of realistic financial goals and plans, and a tendency to equate faith with naïve optimism (God will magically work this out somehow) are all too common. These problems inevitably spread to other sectors of the pastor's life—increased marital and family stress, hopelessness that leads to a toxic mix of depression and resentment, tension between the pastor and the financial decision-makers in the church, fearfulness about alienating the big givers in the church, and mild to extreme ethical lapses as pastors cut corners to make ends meet. Chronic financial stress inevitably creates debilitating levels of unhealthy and distracting self-concern.

In the face of these pressures, it is crucial that pastors find a firm footing regarding their personal finances. The Three Principles suggest ways of doing exactly this. The First Principle invites the pastor to be explicit and intentional about Self, Role, and the intersection between them. It is essential that the pastor remember that he or she is a Self and not just a Role. As self-care literature frequently points out, God cares about who we are and not just what we do on God's behalf. Our personal well-being matters, and our personal well-being includes our financial well-being. It is no accident that Economic Security, Integrity, and Abundance are the second of the eleven areas on the "Grade Yourself" exercise (Appendix A). Only physical well-being ranks higher. Realizing that one aspect of our Self is our Financial Self, we need to include that Financial Self in our self-reflection.

Sara Day, who has counseled many pastors in the American Baptist Churches USA regarding their finances, says that the beginning point for financial wellness is understanding one's financial story. What assumptions about money did you learn in your family of origin? What did your spouse learn in his or her family? What does your theology and spirituality say about money? Deep honesty in probing these questions can be painful, but also freeing. For example, the guilt that motivates many pastors in ministry often also poisons their approach to finances, bringing in unhealthy or unrealistic "spiritual" assumptions about money management. Letting go of that guilt enables realism and frees pastors to take healthy responsibility for their Financial Selves.

This unflinching and courageous commitment to honesty leads naturally to increased clarity about one's current financial reality. Rather than seeking to protect themselves through vagueness and denial, pastors can look honestly at their income, their expenses, and their debt. You may tell yourself that you are "not a numbers person" and cannot understand these matters. Genuinely caring for one's Self requires moving beyond that self-limiting definition by getting whatever help is needed to understand those realities and work through any shame, guilt, or fear that interferes with clear vision. If you struggle in this area, consider developing a positive operational belief that can help you care for your Financial Self. Perhaps you tell yourself: "I learned Greek and Hebrew; I can learn to read a spreadsheet" or "I respect myself; I will show it by directly facing the financial part of my life" or "I will choose to engage the financial part of my life wholeheartedly, in the same way that I engage my ministry wholeheartedly." Just as you benefit from taking the best possible course of action you can imagine in your Role as pastor, so will you also benefit from taking the best possible course of action you can imagine in your functioning as a Self, including your Financial Self.

This brings us to the next phase of developing financial well-being: moving beyond insight and into intention. Financial counselors advise people to have clear financial goals and set their plans to move toward them. In the language of this book, you develop specific intentions that align with your core values, you declare your intentions to others, and you invite people to evaluate you by your commitment to those intentions. Conversations with your spouse and other family members, as appropriate, are a positive way for you to voice your intentions and to hear others voice their own. The Second Principle, which calls pastors to take the strongest position and action they can imagine, speaks well to this phase. Strength is expressed by owning responsibility, while weakness is revealed in blaming others and implicitly claiming helplessness. Rather than passively imagining that things will work out on their own, you begin to set and meet your own goals with God's help. Your first goals will probably be modest: balancing your checkbook, keeping track of what you spend, or putting twenty dollars in your savings account. You may set an intention to make generous giving to others a regular practice. It is more energizing and motivating to set tangible goals you can achieve than to set grand goals that are mere wishful thinking. As your confidence grows, more ambitious and longer-range goals will become realistic options.

Intentions move us into action. Strength is taking action, while weakness is brooding, worry, and passivity. Again, the first steps of action might be relatively simple, as you push forward toward your goals. Having regular family meetings, putting money into savings, or balancing your checkbook are action steps that contribute to your overall well-being as well as your financial health. Simply taking action is good in itself; seeing it have a positive effect is even better. Seeing your indebtedness shrink because you took positive steps is deeply validating. Making sacrifices such as cutting back on expenses or taking on additional work will feel less onerous when it is part of a plan that you have freely chosen. You can feel good about rather than deprived by your decision to have a meal at home rather than eating out because you know that your actions are consistent with your intentions. These short-term actions will lead you toward longer-term decisions and actions that may involve significant changes in lifestyle and/or vocation. As you go through this process, you will come to a stronger faith rooted in personal integrity, honesty, and commitment. Since the best parts of our Selves flow readily into our pastoral Role, you may find that you are finally ready to preach about money in a way that is deeply authentic and rings true to your congregants.

Exercise

Which of these two topics—social media or financial management—left you feeling more uncomfortable? Now can be a time for you to resolutely move toward "troubled waters" by facing that topic and doing some serious reflecting. Choose to be unflinchingly honest with yourself about your discomfort. What aspects of yourself would you prefer to keep vague or out of sight? Let them come into view and begin to work on specific intentions regarding them. Share your intentions with your inner coach as well as with one trustworthy person who is willing to hold you accountable. Then notice how you begin to feel genuinely better about yourself!

CHAPTER 17

Commitment, Momentum, and Beyond

As we come to the end of this book, it's now up to you. I hope that you are ready to make a commitment to the Principles of Excellence. While making that decision is easy, following through in the long-term is not. You need something specific to keep momentum going, especially as you discover that the Principles are not just to be applied to ministry but to your whole life.

Commitment

If you have already decided to adopt the Principles of Health and Excellence, or even if you are considering trying them, this chapter is especially for you. If not, I would invite you—*urge* is a better word—to contact me or any of my colleagues who have worked with me on this project. Appendix B at the back of the book tells you how. I would still suggest that you read on a little further because a commitment to the Principles, though significant and serious, is not all that difficult—either to make or to stick with.

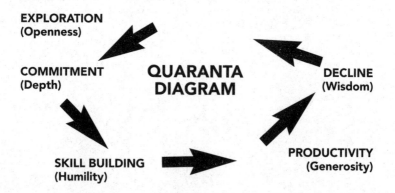

EXPLORATION (Openness)

COMMITMENT (Depth)

QUARANTA DIAGRAM

DECLINE (Wisdom)

SKILL BUILDING (Humility)

PRODUCTIVITY (Generosity)

The Quaranta Diagram places commitment in a context. It is a simple diagram that I learned at a workshop led by Dr. Joseph Quaranta, an Ohio State University professor. The diagram defines the progression of natural stages of any complex human endeavor (exploration, commitment, skill building, productivity, decline). It can be used to locate what is going on in a courtship and marriage, in a pastorate, even in a course on adopting the Principles of Health and Excellence. The cycle is continuous. It does not need to stop when it comes to *decline* or *failure*. It can move from there to *exploration* and start all over again. Beneath the title of each stage is a word that states the value that is most important to the stage—the value that, if attended to diligently, assures the best completion of that stage and gives a strong boost to the subsequent stage. Each stage is valuable to keep in mind as we proceed in ministry. When working with clients, I ask them to identify the stage they're in currently and then focus their excellence on the value related to that stage.

Let's focus on the stage of commitment. The value for commitment is *depth*, and, as we shall see, its meaning has much in common with the *depths* we have been discussing. Commitments come in all sizes and shapes. For certain, there are shallow commitments. There are even pseudo or false commitments, which are quite common. They occur when we commit ourselves to doing something—or at least pretend to—because someone else wants us to, or because everyone else is doing it. Those are commitments detached from what we really want. The fact is, the shallow and false commitments are the hardest to keep. The deepest commitments, on the other hand, are the easiest to keep.

Charlene

When I think of a deep commitment, I think of one of my brightest and best clients. Charlene had about as rough a start in life as anyone I've ever known. Her mother died at age thirteen—not when Charlene was thirteen, but when her mother was. From that point on she was tossed around from one uncaring set of relatives to another, taken advantage of, and suffered every form of abuse imaginable. By age eight she was living in poverty with a grandmother whose paycheck she had to steal so that she could buy food for them both. Otherwise, as she had learned, it would be spent entirely on alcohol. If ever a life was destined to end up on the trash heap, it was hers. Yet when I met her, she was a professional woman who had earned a Ph.D. degree and risen to a high-level position in academic administration at a prestigious university. She had made a decision in her early teens—a commitment to herself—that her life would be totally opposite what she had known up to that point. She had obviously kept that commitment. Equally as remarkable to me, she was now making a second commitment to take another one-hundred-and-eighty degree turn in her life. To carry out her first commitment, she had to develop and maintain a hard edge. She now wanted to live out a softer, more caring side that she knew was there. And to her, that meant pursuing ministry.

Making the commitment she made as a young girl was relatively easy for Charlene. She began with two things she found in her own depths: the notion that she was responsible for herself and had a right to shape her own destiny, and the belief that, no matter the odds, "where there's a will, there's a way." Given those two factors (which you can no doubt find in your own depths), the choice she made was a no-brainer. Life wasn't easy for her, but because of the depth of her commitment, I seriously doubt that she ever—not for one moment—looked back.

Affirming Who You Are Now

In all probability, the changes you will need to make to follow the Principles do not begin to compare with the changes Charlene planned for her life. For some of you, the changes may be very slight. It could even be the case that the only thing that may have kept *you* from being one of my top clients is that our paths haven't crossed. In any case, nothing in what the Principles require for you to get started is terribly difficult. Let's look first at what you are *not* being asked to do. You are not being asked to be someone else. You being *you* makes a far more effective package than you trying to be Colin or Brian or Charlene. In fact, the starting point of this commitment is to affirm yourself as you are—up to the minute, including your decision to follow the Principles. As you have probably learned by now, the first thing you need to do if you are trying to change the culture of a community of people is to *accept* the people where they are. Imagine the self-styled change agent going into a church and saying, "You people are doing it all wrong. You have to change." How far does that person get?

The same is true of the changes you are setting out to make: your best start is to accept and affirm who you are now. One of the implications of this has to do with how fast you attempt to travel on this road to excellence. I would encourage you to start slowly. Take a few steps. Work on letting go of your self-concerns as you start your workday in ministry. Start trying to move into your depths, where you think more clearly and see important things you didn't see before. Start to develop a relationship with your inner coach. Have your coach remind you to ask yourself the question, "Do any of the Rules of Strength apply to this situation I am in?" Note when you start to judge someone, and then imagine yourself letting go of that judgment. Then, just before you go to sleep, ask God for help in letting go so that God can meet you in the depths of your sleep and bestow love on you. None of that is difficult, and all of that together constitutes a great start.

Another reason for starting slowly: if you don't, it will look like you are trying to be someone else. Your children may become scared, your friends dismayed, your congregation confused! If you try to apply all twelve of the Rules of Strength at one time, it may be a train wreck. Making the commitment and starting out slowly may be relatively easy, but what about keeping it? I hope that, like Charlene, yours is a deep commitment. I hope that it is important to you to be as good at what you are doing as you can be. This is not one of those "I don't have anything else to do today, so I think I'll do some excellent ministry" sorts of commitment. Rather it is a commitment that says, "I know the person I want to be in ministry. I know that I'm in charge of what I will be, and I know that I can do it."

In addition, you'll see some immediate benefits that will make you glad, and keep you glad, that you have made this commitment. When you let go of self-concern and feel the resulting lightness in your day, when you surprise someone with your use of one of the Rules of Strength, when you notice how kind you feel toward yourself after you have withdrawn your judgment of another, and even when you face challenges and feel the excitement and sense the meaning of it, you will have no interest in looking back.

Momentum

Even if making the commitment to follow the Principles of Health and Excellence is not difficult, and even if following them provides its own momentum, it is good to have an outside source of momentum, too. Change inevitably creates stress, and if stress becomes great enough, people generally react by regressing—by reverting to earlier, more childlike ways of coping. If that happens, following the Principles falls by the wayside. To keep that from occurring, I always strongly recommend establishing a working relationship with an accountability partner.

An accountability partner is someone you meet with on a regular basis both for support and, of course, accountability. Ideally, it is someone who is also working on the Principles, though it could be someone who is following some other course of self-improvement. You should consider several factors. The first one is your choice of partner. It needs to be someone with whom almost 100 percent of your contact takes place only in your accountability meetings. This eliminates the danger of conflict of interest. It also, of course, disqualifies family members, members of your church, coworkers, and probably best friends. You need to choose someone who cares about you—and especially cares that you succeed in your quest—and who is also tough enough to speak plainly to you and confront you. Beyond that, chemistry is also important; it is helpful to be working with someone you enjoy being with.

Where should you meet and how often? I recommend that you not meet in either of your work environments. Your business together is too important to risk distractions or interruptions. A retreat center is ideal. In any case, it needs to be in a place where there is quiet and privacy. Comfortable is good, too. If you want to share a meal together when you meet, enjoy the meal but do not work on the accountability agenda until afterwards (unless you do it before). That agenda deserves complete focus. I've also had the experience of ordering my favorite dish, but then becoming so engrossed in the business at hand that I later looked down, saw an empty plate, and realized I hadn't been aware of eating it!

How often you meet will depend on circumstances. If you live far from each other, it makes sense to meet less often but for a longer period of time. At the beginning, I usually advise people to not go longer than a month between meetings. Every two weeks is better. Over time you will get a sense of what works best for you. The length of each session will depend on your circumstances, though ninety minutes seems to be a reasonable and productive period.

During the accountability meetings, stick to your purpose. Note that wandering off onto a different topic is probably a sign that you are avoiding something. Know from the beginning that those are probably the most important things to talk about. Undoubtedly the accountability sessions will be of most benefit to you when you talk together about the moments when things did not seem to go well as opposed to spending the most time talking about your successes. Make sure the time is equally divided. Even if one of you had a troubling crisis while the other had a relatively smooth time during the interim, it is important to keep the focus equally divided with respect to time. There is bound to be an inequality in the distribution of crises between you, but that should not affect the equal distribution of time allotted to each of you.

You should have no difficulty finding the appropriate things to talk about. It is helpful to keep a journal as you are working on the Principles and to bring the journal with you. For instance, when you are taking the time to put self-concern behind in your ministry, journal your thought process on at least one occasion. Later, share that with your accountability partner. Similarly, when you are focusing on deciding what is the very best action you can take, again journal your thought process, and later journal what happened when you carried out your decision. Don't be stingy with your affirmations of each other, but do not stint on pushing each other to go further down the road to excellence.

One more word about accountability: it is crucial to be transparent about what you are doing. If congregants and others around you know your intent, they are more aware of what adjustments they might need to make in terms of their expectations of you. They also may get some clues about how to help you, including keeping you accountable. This is different, obviously, from what goes on with your accountability partner, which is focused and systematic. But it also has the advantage that those around you have first-hand knowledge and experience of what you are doing. Also, what you are doing may rub off on them. It is very important to let the lay leaders of the church, who work alongside you, know your intent. When they too begin to act with excellence, things can move faster and further in the church.

I personally prefer the idea of waiting a while before letting the congregation know what you are intending regarding your commitment to excellence. Get a feel yourself first for how it is going. It is much better to hear, "Oh, so that's why she has been doing that" than, "He's planning on doing *what?* Fat chance that will ever happen!"

Beyond

By now it should be clear that the Principles of Health and Excellence are not some trade secret for the eyes of clergy alone. But we haven't said enough about how much they apply to your life apart from ministry—to *beyond* your ministry. This includes both your off-work time—when you're done for the day—and your eventual retirement. Up to now the question has been: "What kind of person in ministry do you want to be?" Now the question is more basic: "What kind of person do you want to be?" The Principles of Health and Excellence will help you with both.

Take the matter of Role, for instance. Up to now, we have been speaking of Role as individual intentional acts based on your decision regarding the best thing you can think of doing for the sake of the effectiveness and integrity of your ministry. Now we are using Role in terms of your overarching status in different Roles. Outside ministry you will still forever have Roles. Much—not all, but much—of your life will be relating to others. And as you do, you will have Roles—parent, spouse, friend, teammate, or temporary comforter to the frazzled store clerk, to name just a few. You are likely to choose your behavior in each of those Roles in such a way that you employ parts of yourself and hold other parts in reserve. Sometimes you will want to make an excellent and unselfish impact because you care about the other person, and you hope that will happen on occasion in these other Roles, too. When it does happen, just as in ministry, you will push self-concern aside and thoughtfully choose the best thing you can do in the moment for the sake of the other.

You will experience a significant difference, however, between excellence in ministry and excellence in life outside ministry. Excellence in ministry requires a steady commitment; in off-work time, you'll have the invitation to commit but not the requirement. You are free in a way that your commitment to ministry does not let you be. One of the best metaphors for excellence is *soaring.* The flight metaphor also is one of the best ways of understanding the difference between excellence in ministry and excellence in "your beyond time" outside ministry. The first is like flying in an airplane, or even piloting the airplane. There is structure. You have a flight plan, a take-off time, schedules to keep, a specific destination, and controls to attend constantly. You are responsible for the safety of a specific group of people. The second is like being a bird, soaring freely through the sky, able to dart into any cove that seems interesting, or to land on any branch that suits your fancy.

In Thornton Wilder's play *Our Town,* an unforgettable moment occurs when Emily, who has died, is permitted to choose one day of her life and come back to experience it. She chooses her twelfth birthday but soon discovers that reliving that good day brings her unexpected pain. l. She laments, "Oh, earth, you're too wonderful for anybody to realize you. Do any human beings every realize life while they live it?—every, every minute?"[1] Does anyone ever realize life every, every minute?" When we consider that Emily's word *realize* has two separate meanings—to be aware of and to fulfill—we can safely answer her question with a no. That would be too much to expect of anyone. If you worry about fulfilling the moment, you will surely defeat your purpose. And what can fulfilling the moment be without bringing God into it? We are back to sea turtle eggs. Maybe if we fulfill one in a thousand or one in two hundred moments, then that is enough. The idea of fulfilling all of them conjures up images of the world being overrun by sea turtles!

We spend much of our off-work time in relationships. Each relationship moment is an opportunity for excellence. Off work we are free to pursue excellence or not. You may be with your kids but engrossed in something that is privately joyful (pursuing a favorite hobby, for instance). At that moment, you are prioritizing yourself and not choosing to strive for excellence in your parenting role. You will have other parenting moments, and besides, your joy is important. Not every moment of every day requires the intentional pursuit of excellence. Sometimes to be relaxed and joyful is the best thing to do for yourself. But remember this: If realizing that the moment involves God, then it also must be about loving one another. And if that is so, your happiness is involved. You may not want to seek excellence in every moment with your kids or with the frazzled store clerk, but your happiness, your ultimate sense of contentment, rests in seeking excellence often and regularly.

I believe that the Principles of Health and Excellence that I have learned from my top clients are, in a real sense, generic. I cannot picture any form of excellence taking place in ministry without some application of putting self-concern behind, acting with real strength, and being motivated by love rather than judgment. Therefore, I believe that each of you has been employing the Principles from time to time. If you think about it and look back on the times of excellence in your life or ministry, you will see that is true. But you might not have known *why* what you did was excellent. Now you know. It is my hope that you will elevate those actions to the level of Principles that will guide your ministry and sprinkle throughout your beyond, so that you will now practice them regularly and experience more and more moments that will be your brightest and best.

Creating a Culture

Let's look at one more application of the notion of "your beyond." Up to now, as we have discussed excellence, we have been looking primarily at individual acts in specific situations: deciding the best thing to do, taking on challenges, taking a position of strength. We have alluded to the possibly disheartening idea that excellence is elusive. You may have done something spectacular one day and fallen flat on your face the next. But, more importantly, as you pursue excellence you are creating something *beyond*, something that is both powerful and enduring. You are creating a *culture*—an atmosphere—around you. And that can be by far the most important thing you do.

Relatively few people create a culture to any significant degree. That can perhaps be demonstrated best by the "what happens when you enter a room" test. What happens when you enter a room occupied by people who know you? There are three possibilities. The most common one is that nothing of a consistent nature happens. The responses vary according to circumstances. You have not created a culture. The second possibility is that, whether spoken or not, people consistently feel: "Oh no! Let me out of here!" You have created a culture, but unfortunately a negative one. The third possibility is that people consistently feel: "I'm so glad you're here." Obviously, you have created a culture, and a very desirable and positive one.

When you conscientiously follow the Health and Excellence road, you create a culture. People are consistently glad to see you for reasons having to do with both health and excellence. They know you as a competent person—one who believes it can be done, one who is accustomed to taking on challenges, one who personifies strength, and one who knows that the tougher the challenge is, the greater the opportunity to grow. They know you as a kind, caring, generous person—one who listens and does not judge, one who forgives, and one who sees the best in others.

I recently stood in line outside a church waiting to join an overflowing crowd at the memorial service for a wonderful young woman in our neighborhood. By any earthly standards, the mood of the service could have been dark and depressing. She might normally have been expected to live another thirty or forty years. Just a week before her death she was a vibrant, joyful, energetic person caring for the environment, social causes, and everyone around her. No one imagined that cancer would claim her life so quickly; no one had time to prepare. While a whole gamut of emotions was expressed during the memorial service, the overwhelming tone was a joyous celebration of a life lived about as well as any life could be. She had, throughout her life, created a culture, and that culture took over even her memorial service. I suspect that almost everyone left that service as I did, feeling more whole and wanting to embrace life in its entirety.

To God belongs all honor and glory. What better thing to be about doing than honoring and glorifying God? And what better way to honor and glorify God, and to please the God who loves you more than you can imagine, than to live your life as well as it can be lived. The road to Health and Excellence is before you. God speed you on your journey!

Exercise

Share with someone your commitment to the Health and Excellence journey and what it's about. Then enjoy a Sabbath!

Note
1. Thornton Wilder, *Our Town: A Play in Three Acts* (New York: Perennial Classics, 2003), 108.

Grade Yourself

Directions: Give a quick, intuitive response to each area of Health listed below. First, however, pay attention to this challenge: Be brave! Be honest! Do not hesitate to give yourself an *F* if it is truly deserved. Nothing here will go on any permanent record. No grade here will keep you out of Harvard Divinity School. Whatever grade you give yourself will be known only to you and whomever you choose to share it with. The challenge is to be scrupulously honest with yourself.

The comments in each of the *Criteria Notes* are intended to be broad definitions only. Consider them alongside your own additional criteria.

PART I

Area 1

THE RHYTHMS OF LIFE
Grade the healthiness of your current way of relating to your own needs (self-care) in each of the following areas.

Sleep   **Your grade** _____
Criteria Notes
Regularly getting an adequate amount of sleep at night; sleeping restfully; minimal amount of waking in the middle of the night; feeling rested and refreshed upon awakening.

Eating   **Your grade** ____

Criteria Notes

Eating nutritionally balanced meals at regular times and under stress-free conditions; rigorously adhering to diet restrictions (whether for medical reasons or personal goals); avoiding excesses in eating or drinking; avoiding compulsive or compensatory eating (eating when anxious, lonely, or depressed).

Exercise   **Your grade** ____

Criteria Notes

Staying physically active and having a consistent, regular exercise program.

Sexual Expression   **Your grade** ____

Criteria Notes

Engaging in behavior that is well-integrated and consistent with your core values; having a sense that your sexuality is a valued and valuable part of who you are; experiencing freedom from guilt; having a sense of ease, comfort, and satisfaction with the extent and frequency of your sexual behavior in marriage, or with your abstinence from sexual behavior if single; having a sense that your sexual expression is fulfilling and enriching to your life and to that of your spouse; recognizing that you are responsible for your sexual conduct in all of your relationships.

*Now grade your overall healthiness in Area 1: The Rhythms of Life.   **Your Grade** ____

Area 2

ECONOMIC SECURITY, INTEGRITY, AND ABUNDANCE
Grade the healthiness of your current ways of relating to your need for economic security, integrity, and abundance.

Economic Security   **Your grade** ____
Criteria Notes
Providing adequately for yourself and those dependent on you; being generally cognizant and in control (through planning and budgeting) of expenditures in the basic expense areas of your life (shelter, food, clothing, health, education, recreation, benevolence, and so on).

Economic Integrity   **Your grade** ____
Criteria Notes
Being scrupulously honest and in line with clearly defined policies in dealing with church funds; living within your means; avoiding excessive debt and inappropriate borrowing; paying off current debts appropriately; resisting materialism; taking responsibility to provide for yourself and your dependents without counting on special clergy benefits (discounts or freebies) or borrowing from the church.

Economic Abundance   **Your grade** ____
Criteria Notes
Finding ways to save (shopping economically, recycling or repurposing items, growing your own food), and, most importantly, cultivating awareness of the gift of grace in what you have and being grateful.

*Now grade your overall healthiness in Area 2: Economic Security, Integrity, and Abundance.   **Your Grade** ____

Area 3

AFFECTION
Grade the healthiness of your current ways of relating to your need for affection.

Affection for Self   Your grade ____
Criteria Notes
Experiencing genuine unreserved care for yourself and your well-being.

Affection for Others   Your grade ____
Criteria Notes
Extending genuine unreserved care for the well-being of others in your life.

Personal Support Network   Your grade ____
Criteria Notes
Identifying specific people whom you can—and *do*—go to when you are hurting; expressing affection both freely and appropriately.

Ability to Accept Praise   Your grade ____
Criteria Notes
Accepting compliments from others appreciatively.

Ability to maintain appropriate boundaries   Your grade ____
Criteria Notes
Managing your own feelings of attraction so that you do not risk fostering inappropriate relationships.

*Now grade your overall healthiness in Area 3: Affection.
                                          Your Grade ____

Area 4

SENSE OF PROFESSIONAL COMPETENCE, INTEGRITY, AND SELF-RESPECT

Grade the healthiness of your ways of relating to your need for a sense of professional competence, integrity, and self-respect.

Professional Competence   Your grade ____
Criteria Notes
Feeling both challenged and fulfilled regularly in what you are doing; finding intellectual stimulation in your work; finding ways to use your creativity in your ministry.

Professional Integrity   Your grade ____
Criteria Notes
Exercising courage in your work; standing strong for your convictions in the face of conflict and opposition.

Professional Self-Respect   Your grade ____
Criteria Notes
Experiencing that what you actually do is consistent with your sense of calling and identity as a minister; carrying out your work in ways that enhance your professional self-respect.

*Now grade your overall healthiness in Area 4: Sense of Professional Competence, Integrity, and Self-Respect.   **Your Grade** ____

Area 5

JOYFUL EXPERIENCE Your grade ____
Grade the healthiness of your ways of relating to your need for joyful experience.
Criteria Notes
Identifying a number of consistent sources of joy in your life; identifying a number of small things that give you joy on a daily basis; taking initiative to seek out those things that bring you joy; letting yourself experience unrestrained joy.

Area 6

SPIRITUAL LIFE AND RELATION TO GOD
Your grade ____
Grade yourself on the healthiness of your ways of relating to your need for spiritual life and relationship with God.
Criteria Notes
Engaging in regular practices to foster your own spiritual life and spiritual development; having a sense of God's presence in your life; feeling buoyed by your spiritual experience and relationship with God; experiencing a sense of peace and gratitude.

PART II

For the next five areas, grade the healthiness of the ways in which you relate to each of these groups of people. While you will have variations within each area, come up with a grade that is generally representative for the area.

Area 7

YOUR PRIMARY GROUP
(SPOUSE, CHILDREN, EXTENDED FAMILY, FRIENDS)

Your overall grade ____

Sub-grades: Spouse ____; Children ____;
Extended Family ____; Friends ____

Criteria Notes

Taking time to be with them, collectively and individually; relating actively to their interests apart from yours; enjoying them for who they are; allowing them to be themselves; being there when they need you; telling them what they mean to you.

Area 8

LEADERS IN THE CONGREGATION

Lay leaders (both official and self-appointed)
Quality of relationship   Your grade ____
Criteria Notes

Establishing and maintaining a trusting relationship with them; communicating clearly your intentions, vision, and work with them; seeking to learn about their intentions, vision, and work; being able to disagree without losing their service or trust.

Transparency   Your grade ____
Criteria Notes

Letting them see the personal you—your faults and shortcomings as well as your positive characteristics.

Positive reinforcement   Your grade ____
Criteria Notes

Affirming them and showing your support.

* Now grade your overall healthiness in Area 8: Leaders in the Congregation. **Your grade** ___

Area 9

PROFESSIONAL COLLEAGUES IN MINISTRY: CHURCH STAFF, DENOMINATIONAL STAFF, PEERS IN MINISTRY

Church Staff   **Your grade** ___
Criteria Notes
Having a clear, mutual understanding of roles in relation to each other; having a clear, mutual understanding of boundaries in your working relationship; respecting each other; affirming them and showing your support; promoting and maintaining a collegial relationship; having a good level of trust and sense of camaraderie; handling differences and conflicts well.

Denominational staff   **Your grade** ___
Criteria Notes
Relating to them as colleagues; trusting them and allowing them to know and trust you; having an understanding of and sensitivity to the responsibilities they carry.

Peers in ministry   **Your grade** ____
Criteria Notes
Regarding other peers in ministry: having a number of relationships in which you both give and receive support for your ministry; acting on a sense of the collegial nature of ministry.

*Now grade your overall healthiness in Area 9: Professional
Colleagues in Ministry: Church Staff, Denominational Staff, Peers
in Ministry.   **Your grade** ____

Area 10

PARISHIONERS/CONSTITUENTS   **Your grade** ____
Criteria Notes
Relating to them equally, without showing favoritism; taking time
to know who they are (to the extent possible); communicating your
intentions, personal policies related to ministry (including boundaries), and the nature of the work you are doing; attempting to gear
your preaching, teaching, and other messages to their personal
worlds; making yourself reasonably available to them; taking initiative to share in their lives; taking initiative to relate to all ages; communicating your interest in their spiritual development and welfare.

Area 11

THE LARGER COMMUNITY   **Your grade** ____
Criteria Notes
Living out, in visible and tangible ways, your sense of being called
to minister to the world, including all of God's children, the environment, and the social/political structure of the community;
showing awareness of local and global concerns; demonstrating
compassion and advocating for justice; practicing non-violence;
and being open to learning from those different than yourself.

Additional Areas Which are Particular to Your Personal or Professional Context

_____

_____ Your grade ____

Criteria Comments:

_____

_____

_____

_____

_____

_____ Your grade ____

Criteria Comments:

_____

_____

_____

_____

Acknowledgments and Contact Information

This Health and Excellence material has come about through the work of a community of people. In addition to myself, my colleagues throughout the Ministry Development Network have been involved both in developing and working with the Principles described in the book. I especially want to thank Kristina Gutiérrez and Ross Peterson for their invaluable collaboration and advice in bringing the Principles into a format that can be shared widely.

My colleagues in the Columbus, Ohio, office are very closely acquainted with the work that has evolved into this book. You can reach them, as well as myself, at the address below. Specifically, Dr. Vickie P. McCreary and Rev. Dr. Kristina R. Gutiérrez would be glad to help you with any matters related to Health and Excellence in ministry. Staff in our Chicago area office, where Dr. Margo M. R. Stone, Rev. J. Christopher Pickett, and Rev. Dr. Ross D. Peterson are located, are also deeply committed to the development of clergy Health and Excellence and are available for individual or group consultations.

Midwest Ministry Development Service
1234 Old Henderson Rd, Suite B / Columbus OH 43220 / (614) 442-8822

Midwest Ministry Development Service
1840 Westchester Blvd, Suite 204 / Westchester IL 60154 / (708) 343-6268

www.midwestministrydev.org
Like us on Facebook @ www.facebook.com/MidwestMinistryDevelopment